THE NATIONAL VOTER REGISTRATION ACT

Impact and Implications for Latino and Non-Latino Communities

Elaine Rodriquez

Foreword by Maurilio Vigil

University Press of America,® Inc.
Lanham · Boulder · New York · Toronto · Plymouth, UK

Copyright © 2009 by
University Press of America,® Inc.
4501 Forbes Boulevard
Suite 200
Lanham, Maryland 20706
UPA Acquisitions Department (301) 459-3366

Estover Road
Plymouth PL6 7PY
United Kingdom

Library of Congress Control Number: 2008938696
ISBN-13: 978-0-7618-4445-7 (paperback : alk. paper)
ISBN-10: 0-7618-4445-7 (paperback : alk. paper)
eISBN-13: 978-0-7618-4446-4
eISBN-10: 0-7618-4446-5

I dedicate this work to my family: to my beautiful and amazing daughter, Danelle Rodriquez-Henderson, who grew up through this process and never once complained, and whose love and hugs comforted and encouraged me; to my loving and supportive parents, Joe Lloyd and Margaret Baca-Rodriquez, who taught me a strong work ethic, persistence, and discipline—characteristics essential to overcoming any challenge; to my husband, Ronald Lucero, who listened to my rants and raves and reassured me that "this too will pass"; and finally, to my aunt, Alvera Rodriquez-Eylea, who shades me with love and inspiration from above.

CONTENTS

LIST OF FIGURES

LIST OF TABLES

FOREWORD

"A man without a vote," President Lyndon B. Johnson once said, "is a man without protection." This quote recognizes the importance of voting in the United States, where public policy is often connected to one's vote. In this country, which prides itself as the birthplace of true democracy, the right to vote has been an illusive privilege. At the time of the founding of the Republic, when such documents as the Declaration of Independence and the U.S. Constitution were formulated and adopted, the suffrage was restricted to white male property owners over the age of twenty-one.

The struggle for true universal suffrage has been a hard-fought battle, with the established powers fighting vigorously to retain their exclusive entitlement. Nevertheless, reforms have been made. Following the Civil War, Black men—former slaves—were formally granted the vote as part of the reforms of the Fifteenth Amendment to the Constitution, although it would take more than a century to fully implement the right. Women gained the right to vote in the Nineteenth Amendment, adopted in 1920, after a protracted and bitter struggle. In more recent times, additional barriers to voting such as poll taxes, literacy tests, and the white primary were eliminated. Still, racially-based discriminatory barriers against Blacks, Latinos, and Native Americans persisted until the 1965 Voting Rights Act. The result of the Voting Rights Act was increased participation, especially among Blacks. In 1971 the Twenty-sixth Amendment extended the right to vote to citizens aged eighteen and older.

Notwithstanding such reforms, exercise of the suffrage has been less than overwhelming in American elections, with just 50 percent to 60 percent of eligible voters participating in presidential elections. Some authorities attribute the low levels of participation to "institutional barriers." The authors of one major textbook, *Government by the People* (2006), James M. Burns et al., argue that one "peculiar American requirement, 'voter registration,' discourages voting." This view is affirmed in a study by Raymond Wolfinger and Steven Rosenstone, *Who Votes* (1980), where they conclude that liberalized registration laws would produce an additional 12.2 million voters and increase participation by 9 percent.

Accordingly, in 1993 the U.S. Congress enacted, and President Bill Clinton signed, the National Voter Registration Act (NVRA), better known as the Motor Voter Bill, so called because it allows people to register to vote while applying for or renewing a driver's license.

The NVRA requires states to designate offices that provide welfare and disability assistance to facilitate voter registration and to allow registration by mail. It specifically targeted states with troublesome records in voter registration and participation, especially as they applied to minority groups such as Latinos, Blacks, and Native Americans. Today, just fifteen years after the enactment of NVRA, the first substantive studies analyzing the impact of the legislation have begun to surface.

The present study, *The National Voter Registration Act: Impact and Implications for Latino and Non-Latino Communities,* by Elaine Rodriquez-Lucero, initially undertaken as her Ph.D. dissertation and continued in the present work, is an important new case study on the impact of the NVRA in Arizona, particularly as it applies to Latinos in that state. Following an extensive historical background on Latino voting behavior in the United States and in Arizona, the study recounts how Arizona, acting both unilaterally and under the mandates and guidelines of the federal NVRA, adopted, as a result of citizen and advocacy group initiatives and state legislative actions, policies implementing motor and liberalized voter registration procedures. Using survey research, interviews, data from a Northern Arizona University multiyear Arizona poll, and some statistical analysis, the study concludes that NVRA-type reforms yielded only marginal success in registering significant numbers of new Latino voters in Arizona. The study finds that Latino voters are more likely to use traditional (non-NVRA) methods to register to vote. NVRA-type reforms are not the proverbial silver bullet solution to Latino non-voting. NVRA is an electoral reform strategy directed at citizens, and since many Latinos are not citizens, they must first become naturalized citizens in order to become fully integrated into the American political process.

The study also contributes new insight to the learning curve regarding procedural problems in administratively implementing NVRA-type reforms. A corollary contribution of the work is its application and critique of Rodney Hero's "two-tiered pluralism" theory of Latinos in the American political system, which has heretofore gone unchallenged. As Rodriquez points out (p. 114), the [two-tiered] model, like previous conceptual frameworks, "treats all Latinos as a homogeneous group, not recognizing historical, structural, socioeconomic, racial, and ethnic differences" inherent in the group. Given that Latinos are one of the most diverse groups in American politics, any attempt to generalize will invariably produce an exception, consequently rendering the model irrelevant.

Happily, the study concludes that as all citizens become more familiar with the new NVRA-type registration procedures, participation in registration and voting does increase. This suggests that as the more liberalized registration procedures become more institutionalized and widely applied across the nation, they will probably generate greater levels of registration and voting by Americans in general and among targeted groups such as Latinos in particular. In the end, the study offers promise that continued policy initiatives, such as NVRA, are beneficial in enabling the United States to achieve true universal suffrage.

Maurilio E. Vigil, Ph.D.
Emeritus Professor of Political Science
New Mexico Highlands University

PREFACE

My interest in Latino suffrage, Latino political participation, and the implication of public policy for Latino communities began as a graduate student under the guidance of Dr. Maurillio Vigil at New Mexico Highlands University and continued at Northern Arizona University, where I acquired public opinion research skills while working with Dr. Frederic I. Solop, director of NAU's Social Research Laboratory. Today I am a visiting professor at New Mexico Highlands University instructing on Latino political behavior.

Understanding the role that Latino communities play in American politics is central to questions regarding minority political behavior in a country marked by arbitrary and exclusionary electoral practices, thus leading to inequitable and unjust outcomes. National legislation like the Voting Rights Act of 1965 and more recently the 1993 National Voter Registration Act (NVRA) were enacted to compensate for past electoral practices of exclusion.

On the surface, Latino political participation presents a dim reality among an increasing Latino population. Yet, underlying the surface, Latino political participation is impeded by recognizable education and income inequality, generational effects, noncitizenship status, and the lack of political resources, which varies considerably among Latino communities in the fifty states. Latino political clout is recognized in barrios and enclaves and regions within cities and counties within important electoral states. Eight of ten Latinos reside in ten states; those states comprise 212 of the 270 electoral votes needed to win the presidential election. With ongoing migration among Latino populations, public policy, like NVRA's motor-voter and mail-in programs, are aimed at encouraging migratory populations to register to vote.

Embarking on an examination of NVRA and its impact enabled this researcher to evaluate the net effects of the National Voter Registration Act on overall voter registration and turnout rates in Arizona, and the consequences ofthis reform for Latino communities.

ACKNOWLEDGEMENTS

I would like to thank Drs. Maurilio Vigil, Frederic I. Solop, Earl Shaw, and David Camacho for mentoring and directing my studies and providing me with support and encouragement to acquire the academic skills and knowledge necessary to pursue a doctoral degree and a professional career in higher education. I also would like to thank Louie Morton, professor at Mesa State College, who recognized my scholastic ability and encouraged me to continue my pursuit of pedagogy.

I would like to thank Arizona's county recorders and public assistance agency managers for their personal interviews, which assisted this researcher in evaluating NVRA programs. Dr. Maurilio Vigil, although retired, agreed to write the foreword, and Chris Potash spent considerable time in reviewing and editing drafts of this book.

A special thank you to my colleagues and comrades Ventris Woods, Eva Barrraza, and Natalina Monteiro for their support, encouragement, and many intellectual discussions and late-night debates. Finally, to *mis amigas* Dolores Pitman-Garcia and Phyllis Galvan for their continuous friendship, support, and encouragement.

INTRODUCTION

> Voting is the most basic form of political participation and a fundamental element of American democracy. The less political participation there is in society, the weaker is the democracy.
> — Greenberg and Page, 1993 —

Since the inception of the National Voter Registration Act (NVRA)[1], voter registration in the United States has remained fairly constant—64 percent for the 1996 and 2000 presidential elections, and 66 percent for the 2004 presidential election. However, voter turnout has steadily increased, from 49 percent in 1996[2] to 55 percent in 2000[3] and 58 percent in 2004. Can the rise in voter turnout be attributed to the National Voter Registration Act?

The passage of the National Voter Registration Act in 1993 mandated all states, except those with election day voter registration or those not requiring voter registration,[4] to implement NVRA measures by January 1, 1995. The objective of the NVRA was to create a voter-registration system that offers eligible citizens alternative methods to register to vote, thereby increasing the number of registered voters and ensuring the likelihood of increased voter turnout. Under the NVRA, individuals can register to vote while applying for a driver's license or public assistance, or by simply completing and returning a mail-in registration form. Moreover, the NVRA allows for "fail-safe" voting procedures[5] and prohibits states from purging[6] registrants for not voting.[7]

The National Voter Registration Act is considered the most progressive electoral reform since the Voter Rights Act of 1965. It was intended to equalize the political playing field by making voter registration and voting less cumbersome to previously disenfranchised groups. It has met with some resistance and criticism, mainly because the election process is considered under the domain of the state and states view federal mandates, especially unfunded mandates such as the NVRA, as an intrusion on their rights. Besides, the much-anticipated increase in voter turnout did not materialize into significant gains in the 1996 presidential election. As a matter of fact, voter turnout in the 1996 presidential election was the lowest in more than 72 years,[8] resulting in whispers of criticism aimed at the NVRA.

Theoretically, the NVRA should increase voter participation among previously excluded populations. In practice, how states implement and administer the NVRA will determine its effectiveness in increasing voter participation among various disenfranchised populations. This book examines whether structural reforms, like the NVRA, afford political access to previously disenfranchised populations by reporting the net effect of the NVRA on overall voter registration rates for Arizona's general community and Latino community, and by responding to the following questions: What works? What doesn't work? And will NVRA registrants actually turn out to cast their vote on Election Day? The reader will gain a greater understanding of the effectiveness of the NVRA as an election-reform strategy when applied to efforts to increase voter registration and turnout rates, and which populations—enfranchised or disenfranchised—are more likely to benefit from the NVRA.

This book offers the following:

- For national and state elected and appointed public officials, an analysis of the changing Latino population and political participation and reachable political clout in key electoral states.

- For state and local administrators, a data-driven analysis of public policy, discovering the real-life net effects and identifying what works and what does not work.

- For reform advocates, community organizers, and Latino special-interest groups, an evaluation of NVRA as an election-reform strategy utilized and applied toward increasing voter registration among various populations.

- For undergraduate and graduate-level students, the applicability of Rodney Hero's theoretical framework of two-tiered pluralism, and the consequences produced by two-tiered pluralism for Latino populations. In addition, the application of quantitative and qualitative methodologies used to examine NVRA can be evaluated, critiqued, and advanced by students in the classroom. Lastly, this work serves as a case study in public policy.

FEDERAL ELECTIONS

Article I of the U.S. Constitution states, "The times, places and manner of holding elections ... shall be prescribed in each state."[9] Roughly 10,000 county or local-level jurisdictions[10] administer the federal election system used to select political leaders and establish public policy. In order for citizens to participate in the electoral process they must register to vote, and they must vote on a designated day. Registering to vote is a prerequisite for voting in all states.

The objective of most U.S. voter registration systems was to reduce multiple voting or voter fraud. The early voter registration laws (1860–1880) were aimed at urban political machines that solicited new immigrants to cast their votes multiple times. To prevent fraudulent voting, time restrictions were established to check the eligibility of prospective voters and their alleged residences. Most U.S. registration laws were passed between the end of Reconstruction and the onset of World War I and were directed at immigrants in the North, blacks and poor whites in the South, and Mexican Americans in the Southwest. These early voter registration laws achieved the goal of decreasing voter turnout.[11]

In the past, institutional practices of election laws (i.e., voter-registration re-strictions) created obstacles that limited individual access to the ballot box. The present structure of election laws continues to be an obstacle to voting. These structural procedures discourage people from becoming involved in the electoral system and are instrumental in disproportionately excluding some groups from the electoral process.[12] The Voting Rights Act of 1965 was enacted to attack the political structural barriers intentionally designed to exclude individuals because of their race, particularly African Americans.[13] Supreme Court cases, such as *Katzenbach v. Morgan* (1966) and *Garza v. Smith* (1970) laid the groundwork for the 1975 amendment to the Voting Rights Act of 1965, which extended pro-tections to language minorities including Puerto Ricans and Mexican Ameri-cans.[14] Again in the 1980s, after studying fifteen states' voting practices, the U.S Commission on Civil Rights found that "registration rates for minorities contin-ued to lag well behind the rates for whites." The Commission concluded:

> among the reasons for the persistence of this disparity were resistance to minor-ity registration by openly hostile local registrars, refusals to allow representa-tives of minority organizations to act as deputy registrars or to establish satellite sites in minority communities, and selective purges or re-registration proce-dures. In addition, the lack of bilingual voter services limited the ability of lan-guage minorities to register to vote.[15]

During deliberations of the 1993 National Voter Registration Act, the 103rd Congress found that:
1. The right of citizens of the United States to vote is a fundamental right;
2. It is the duty of the federal, state, and local governments to promote the exercise of that right; and
3. Discriminatory and unfair registration laws and procedures can have a direct and damaging effect on voter participation in elections for feder-al office and disproportionately harm voter participation by various groups, including racial minorities.[16]

So if the history of voting rights in the United States is used as the standard of measurement in evaluating how effective states have been in creating an in-clusive electoral system that promotes increased voter participation, we can de-duce that states' election laws were somewhat restrictive and have sluggishly relaxed many of their electoral laws over the past forty years. It has been pre-dicted that voter registration reforms, such as motor-voter registration, mail-in registration, agency-based registration, and fail-safe provisions, would equalize representation and produce a political system more widely accessible to a pre-viously disenfranchised public.

THE DISENFRANCHISED PUBLIC:
WHO ARE THE NONVOTERS?

Political scientists and sociologists have conducted numerous studies identifying demographic characteristics that distinguish the voting population from the non-voting population. The people least likely to vote are individuals who are social-ly disconnected—younger, unemployed, or those who have lower incomes, rent their homes, have fewer years of formal education, or are of minority heritage.[17] Studies have found that members of minority groups are less politically active nationally than members of nonminority groups.[18] More specifically, Latinos are less likely than Whites and African Americans to participate in electoral[19] and non-electoral[20] political activities.[21] In *Voice and Equality* (1995), Sidney Verba, Kay Lehman Schlozman, and Henry E. Brady compared political activity among Whites, African Americans, Latinos,[22] and Latino citizens[23] in the United States and found that Latino respondents were less politically active than Whites and Afri-can Americans.[24]

The disparity in electoral and nonelectoral political activities between Whites, African Americans, and Latinos subsides when considering only Latino citizens (the mean score for Latinos rises from 1.2 to 1.4).[25] Moreover, Latinos are not a homogeneous group. Their electoral behavior varies among the various sub-groups—Mexican Americans, Puerto Ricans, Dominicans, and Cubans.[26] Just "being Black or Latino" does not create the participation gap between the differ-ent racial and ethnic groups.[27] The predominant factors associated with low le-vels of civic participation in Latinos are the socioeconomic makeup of the community and the various political skills Latinos acquire and apply to the polit-ical process.[28]

TWO-TIERED PLURALISM:
LATINOS AND THE POLITICAL SYSTEM

Political scientist Rodney Hero explains that Latinos' exclusion from the politi-cal process is a function of two-tiered pluralism. According to Hero, Latinos encounter "a situation in which there is formal legal equality on the one hand, and simultaneously, actual practice that undercuts equality for most members of minority groups."[29]

Hero's theoretical concept of two-tiered pluralism describes Latino politics within the framework of power. He proposes that for Latinos, democracy operates under a dual pluralistic political system. The first tier of the dual pluralistic political process operates based on the U.S. Constitution, treaties, state constitutions, and local laws that guarantee American citizens fundamental constitutional rights and liberties, such as the right to vote and "formal equality." The second tier of the dual pluralistic political process operates based on "applied/informal" governmental procedure.[30] Practices systematically structured into the normal day-to-day opera-tion of all American institutions undercut equality and create a limited real equality for many Latinos.

Formal/legal rights are essential to political power and decision-making processes. Devoid of these formal rights, one's political and decision-making power is severely restricted.[31] According to Hero, few Latinos gain inclusion into the first tier, which suggests that few participate in the development and allocation of public policy.[32] The vast majority of Latinos are concentrated in the second tier of two-tiered pluralism and are more likely to be the recipient of policies that relegate Latinos to the status of client and not active citizen.[33]

The consequences of two-tiered pluralism are that Latinos are more likely to be dealt with through mediating institutions, such as welfare bureaucracies, most often by street-level bureaucrats and nonprofit organizations, whereas dominant groups deal directly with governments through clientele agencies or with those at the top.[34] This system limits Latino political and social access and influence and diminishes Latino political status within the U.S. political system.[35] Hero concludes that due to "historical, socioeconomic, and other factors, minority individuals and groups have largely been relegated to a lower social and political tier or arena."[36] Seldom, he says, does Latino political influence reach parity with that of non-Latinos, even if from time to time individual Latinos achieve political victories. Collectively, "Latinos and Latino politics have been relegated to a lesser place in the U.S. political system."[37]

In other words, for many Latinos, especially those who are less educated and in the lower stratum of the socioeconomic ladder, the United States operates under a facade of democratic principle. Certain institutions that claim to foster democratic participation among American citizens have the opposite effect, that of denying political opportunities for Latinos.

METHODOLOGICAL APPROACH TO THE STUDY

Studies conducted between the 1970s and 1990s measuring the effect of electoral reform on voter turnout used quantitative methodological designs and theoretically concluded that reforming voter registration laws should increase voter turnout rates anywhere from 7.6 percent to 14 percent[38] In Arizona, reforming the voter registration laws could possibly increase voter turnout by 13.6[39] percent and 14.3 percent.[40] At best, these studies offered speculative results on voter turnout rates. This study focuses on the applied or "real-life" net effect of the NVRA, by observing and evaluating the actual practice of the NVRA in Arizona as opposed to the hypothetical or speculative effect of electoral reform. Utilizing a mixed methodological approach—a case-study approach combined with attitudinal data gained from surveys—in a triangulating fashion offers a more comprehensive inquiry rendering answers to the following questions:

1. Which methods of registration—traditional (non-NVRA) methods or reformed (NVRA-type) methods[41]—were registrants more likely to access to register to vote?
2. Which demographic groups—based on race/ethnicity, income, education, age, and party affiliation—are significant indicators of who is

likely to register through traditional (non-NVRA) methods or reformed (NVRA-type) methods of registration?

3.   What is the likelihood that individuals registering through reformed (NVRA-type) methods of registration actually turn out to vote on Election Day?

4.   How are the NVRA reforms being implemented, and how does the process of implementation target previously disenfranchised populations, specifically the Latino community?

5.   How successful have the NVRA-type reforms been in achieving the objective of increasing the number of Latino registrants?

ORGANIZATION OF THE CHAPTERS

Chapter one describes and examines American political participation, voter registration, and voter turnout data within a macrocosmic setting by comparing U.S. voter turnout to that of other industrialized republics, and then narrows the discussion and analysis to the Western states and finally to a microcosmic single-case study of Arizona.

Why Arizona? Before the election-reform movement, "Arizonans faced so many barriers to the ballot," activists say, "that it's a wonder anyone gets registered, let alone votes."[42] On a state-by-state analysis, Arizona has one of the most regressive sets of registration laws in the United States.[43] Ruy Teixeira, in *The Disappearing American Voter* (1992), concluded that electoral reform would have a "more significant" impact in Arizona than in most other states and projected that if Arizona reformed its election laws, voter participation would increase by 13.7 percent.[44] The chapter continues with a discussion of survey data on the demographic characteristics of "likely voters" and "unlikely voters" with an emphasis on Latino and Latino citizen populations. The chapter concludes with scholastic explanations for low voter participation, socio-psychological and legal-institutional factors, and the projected effects "liberalized registration laws" would have on voter turnout.

Chapter two examines political participation among the Latino population and the Latino citizen population. It contrasts Latino citizen voting rates with non-Latino populations. In examining Latino political participation, the book necessarily differentiates the overall Latino population from the Latino citizen population because only citizens can vote.

While the focus in chapter two is on the Latino citizen population, it is necessary to analyze this group within the broader context because of its potential for growth and political clout of the Latino community in key electoral states. This book does not neglect the noncitizen Latino population, because they are an integral part of the growing electoral potential of the overall Latino population, and because public policy impacts citizens and noncitizens alike. This chapter provides a profile of Latino "likely voters" and nonvoters and comparatively examines the socio-economic characteristics of the Latino population and non-Latino population. Also, as indicated in chapter one, low socioeconomic status indicators account for nonparticipation among American citizens.

In chapter two, socioeconomic characteristics are examined to determine if the Latino population mirrors many low socioeconomic factors that have accounted for nonvoting among American citizens. In addition, the chapter provides a comprehensive survey of Latino political participation, beginning with the incorporation of Mexican citizens into the American political system. The treaty of Guadalupe Hidalgo became the starting point for formal relations between Mexican Americans, the largest Latino ethnic group, and the U.S. political system. The chapter concludes by describing the research setting—the Latino population and Latino political participation in Arizona.

Chapter three highlights the movement to reform Arizona's voter registration and election laws over the span of two decades—the 1980s and the 1990s. It provides insight into the many political actors and influences that interacted with one another to sway governmental institutions to act or to refrain from acting on the shaping of Arizona's current election laws. The chapter discusses the implementation of the National Voter Registration Act in Arizona and concludes by examining the potential impact of Arizona election reforms.

Chapter four provides a qualitative assessment on the day-to-day operation and performance of Arizona's voter registration programs, while highlighting NVRA-type reforms. Chapter four also offers a comparative analysis between traditional (non-NVRA) and reform (NVRA-type) methods of voter registration using a compilation of five statewide telephone surveys conducted with 2,148 adult residents of Arizona, of which 10 percent or 215 of the respondents were of Latino heritage. Chapter four examines which demographic groups are more likely to register through reformed voter registration programs, and it concludes with an analysis of the relationship between voter registration methods and voter turnout in the 1992 and 1994 elections.

Chapter five reports the effects of the 1993 National Voter Registration Act on overall voter registration and turnout rates in Arizona, and the consequences of this reform for Latino communities. The chapter provides answers to the following questions: 1) Which NVRA-type methods are Arizonans more likely to access? 2) Who is taking advantage of NVRA?, and 3) How successful have NVRA-type reforms been in achieving its objective? It concludes with a discussion of NVRA as an election-reform strategy to equalize the playing field.

NOTES

1. House, *Public Law 103-31*, 103d Congress, 1st Session, 1993, 107 Stat 77–89.
2. United States, "National Voter Turnout in Federal Elections: 1960–1996," *Federal Election Commission* [Government database]; available from http://www.fed.gov/pages /htmlto5.htm, Internet; accessed 24 February 1997.
3. "Presidential Election Voter Turnout: 1924–2000," *The Center for Voting and Democracy*, http://www.fairvote.org/turnout/preturn.htm.
4. Election-day registration refers to the process whereby an individual would be able to register and vote on election day. States enacting election-day registration and exempt from the NVRA are Minnesota, Wisconsin, Wyoming, Idaho, and New Hampshire. North Dakota is the only state that does not require voters to register.
5. "Fail-safe" provisions guarantee that registrants will not be denied their right to vote due to bureaucratic or legal technicalities.
6. A process whereby registered voters are removed from the registration rolls because they failed to vote in a general election.
7. See: U.S. Congress, Federal Election Commission Report. "The Impact of the National Voter Registration Act of 1993 on the Administration of Elections for Elected Office, 1993–1994," July 1995; Council of State Governments, *The National Voter Registration Act of 1993 Manual* (Lexington, KY, 1994), pp. 1–15.
8. Royce Crocker, Royce, *Voter Registration and Turnout: 1948–1992* (Washington, D.C.: Congressional Research Service, Library of Congress, 1994).
9. The United States Constitution, Article 1, Section 4, Clause 1.
10. Eric A. Fisher, "Voting Technologies in the United States: Overview and Issues for Congress," *CRS Report* RL30773 (pdf), 21 March 2001.
11. Kevin P. Phillips and Paul H. Blackman, *Electoral Reform and Voter Participation* (Washington, D.C.: American Enterprise Institute for Public Policy Research, 1975), pp. 7–8.
12. Frances Fox Piven and Richard A. Cloward, *Why Americans Don't Vote* (New York: Pantheon Books, 1988), pp. 96–112.
13. Phillips and Blackman, *Electoral Reform and Voter Participation*, p. 10.
14. Voting Rights Act, "Timeline," www.votingrights.org/timeline; and Reynaldo A. Valencia and Others, *Mexican Americans and the Law*, pp. 115–116.
15. Commission on Civil Rights, *Barriers to Registration and Voting: An Agenda for Reform* (Washington, D.C.: Citizen's Commission on Civil Rights, 1988), pp. 101–102.
16. House, *Public Law 103–31*, p. 77.
17. Ruy Teixeira, *The Disappearing American Voter*, pp. 58–105; Raymond E. Wolfinger and Steven J. Rosenstone, *Who Votes?*, pp. 13–60; and M. Margaret Conway, *Political Participation in the United States* (Washington, D.C.: Congressional Quarterly Inc., 1991), pp.15–36.
18. Sideny Verba and Norman H. Nie, *Participation in America* (New York: Harper and Row, 1972), p. 162; Raymond E. Wolfinger and Steven J. Rosenstone, *Who Votes?*, pp. 90–91; and Ruy Teixeira, *The Disappearing American Voter*, pp. 71–72.

19. Electoral forms of participation are voting, trying to influence how others vote, attending political meetings or rallies, working for a political party or candidate, contributing money to a party/candidate or PAC.

20. Nonelectoral forms of participation are writing a congressman, signing a petition, attending a public meeting, serving on a committee for a local club, serving as an officer of a club, belonging to a political club, belonging to a group for better government.

21. See Maria Antonia Calvo and Steven J. Rosenstone, *Hispanic Political Participation* (San Antonio, TX: Southwest Voter Research Institute, 1989), pp. 2–3; and see also Sidney Verba et al., "Race, Ethnicity, and Political Resources: Participation in the United States," *British Journal of Politics 23* (1993): pp. 459–466; and Sidney Verba, Kay Lehman Schlozman and Henry E. Brady, *Voice and Equality* (Massachusetts: Harvard University Press, 1995), pp. 231–233.

22. Based on Latino voting-age population.

23. Latino citizens, native born and naturalized.

24. Sidney Verba, Kay Lehman Schlozman, and Henry E. Brady, *Voice and Equality* (Massachusetts: Harvard University Press, 1995), pp. 231–239.

25. Ibid., p. 231.

26. Rodolfo O. De la Garza et al., *Latino Voices* (Colorado: Westview Press, 1992), pp. 113–120; and Sidney Verba, Kay Lehman Schlozman and Henry E. Brady, *Voice and Equality* (Massachusetts: Harvard University Press, 1995), pp. 231–232.

27. Sidney Verba, Kay Lehman Schlozman and Henry E. Brady, *Voice and Equality* (Massachusetts: Harvard University Press, 1995), p. 523.

28. Ibid., p. 523.

29. Rodney Hero, *Latinos and the U.S. Political System* (Philadelphia: Temple University, 1992), pp. 189–190.

30. Ibid., pp. 189–192.

31. Ibid,, p. 191.

32. Ibid., p. 196.

33. Ibid., p. 195.

34. Ibid., p. 193.

35. Ibid., pp. 29, 63.

36. Ibid., p. 29.

37. Ibid., pp. 29–30.

38. Steven J. Rosenstone and Raymond E. Wolfinger, "The Effect of Registration Laws on Voter Turnout," *The American Political Science Review 72* (1978): pp. 32–36; Ruy Teixiera, *The Disappearing American Voter*, p. 114; Staci Rhine, "Registration Reform and Turnout in the American States," *American Politics Quarterly 23* (1995): pp. 419–421; "Registration Reform and Its Relationship to Turnout in the American States," Ph. D. dissertation (1993): p.184; and Glenn E. Mitchell and Christopher Wlezein, "The Impact of Legal Constraints on Voter Registration, Turnout, and the Composition of the American Electorate," *Political Behavior* (1995): pp. 118–191.

39. Ruy Teixiera, *The Disappearing American Voter*, p. 116.

40. Mitchell and Wlezein, "The Impact of Legal Constraints on Voter Registration, Turnout, and the Composition of the American Electorate," pp. 189–190.

41. Keep in mind that Arizona had already implemented many of the federally mandated NVRA programs and only had to tweak their voter registration programs to comply with the NVRA. The term "NVRA-type methods of voter registration" is used interchangeably with "Arizona's reformed methods of voter registration," just to distinguish between reformed methods and traditional or non-NVRA methods of voter registration.

42. Steve Yozwiak, "Registering: Bump on Road to Polls 'Motor Voter' Helps Expand Rolls Election," *The Arizona Republic,* 16 July 1990, A1.

43. Ruy Teixiera, *The Disappearing American Voter,* p. 116.

44. Ibid., p. 116.

CHAPTER ONE

AMERICAN POLITICAL PARTICIPATION

> The United States is the only major democracy where government assumes no
> responsibility for helping citizens cope with voter registration procedures. The
> result is a pronounced class bias to our democracy.
> —Frances Piven and Richard Cloward, 1988—

The paradox of political participation in the United States is that the participation of American citizens in conventional politics has remained fairly consistent over time, with the exception of voting.[1] Despite the progress being made in reducing restrictive practices in the electoral system and the continuous rise in educational levels,[2] voter turnout over the last several decades has continued to drop.

This chapter discusses American political participation in voting within a macrocosmic setting—comparing U.S. voter turnout to that of other industrialized republics—then narrows the discussion to a microcosmic single-case study of Arizona. This is followed by a descriptive and comparative analysis of who votes, and concludes with an empirical understanding of the causes of declining voter participation rates in the United States and in Arizona.

INTERNATIONAL ELECTION PROCEDURES AND VOTER TURNOUT

When comparing this nation's voter turnout to that of other democratized nations, the United States is positioned in the bottom quintile—ranked 138 out of 169 countries—averaging only 47.7 percent voter turnout over 28 presidential and midterm elections (see Appendix A).[3] Some democracies, such as Italy, Iceland, Portugal, New Zealand, Belgium, Austria, Australia, and Sweden, have high turnout rates ranging from 92 percent to 84 percent, while other democracies, such as Columbia, Botswana, and the United States, experience turnout rates below 50 percent. Ten of the thirty-six established democracies—Italy, Belgium, Austria, Australia, Netherlands, Greece, Costa Rica, France, Luxembourg, and Switzerland—have compulsory voting laws that mandate its citizens to vote in a general election. Sanctions for not voting range from fines to incarceration or "innocuous sanction."[4] More than two-thirds (twenty-four) of the established democracies have compulsory voter registration, and about one-half of the countries have some form of state initiated voter registration system whereby the government automatically registers its citizenry. For example, Australia has strict compulsory voter laws, door-to-door registration, mobile election registrars, internet registration, and a system that creates and maintains voter registration information by linking to government services.

Clearly, countries with strict compulsory voter laws, enforced compulsory voter registration, and state-initiated voter registration systems average higher electoral turnout rates than countries with voluntary systems. For this reason, state initiated and federally mandated voter registration programs, such as the National Voter Registration Act, were enacted in the United States.

ELECTION-DAY TURNOUT IN THE UNITED STATES

Since 1960 this nation has experienced a steady decline in voter turnout. As illustrated in figure 1.1, the rate of voter turnout in the United States dropped 13 percentage points from 1960 to 1988. For the 1992 presidential election, turnout increased to 55 percent, the highest rate in more than twenty years, hinting at a possible return to election turnout rates similar to the 1950s and 1960s. However, only 49 percent of Americans voted in the 1996 presidential election—the lowest number in more than seventy-two years. In order to resurrect American voter turnout, the U.S. Census Bureau began reporting voter turnout rates based on the voting-age citizen population.

FIGURE 1.1
U.S. and Citizen Voter Turnout in Presidential Elections:
1948 to 2004

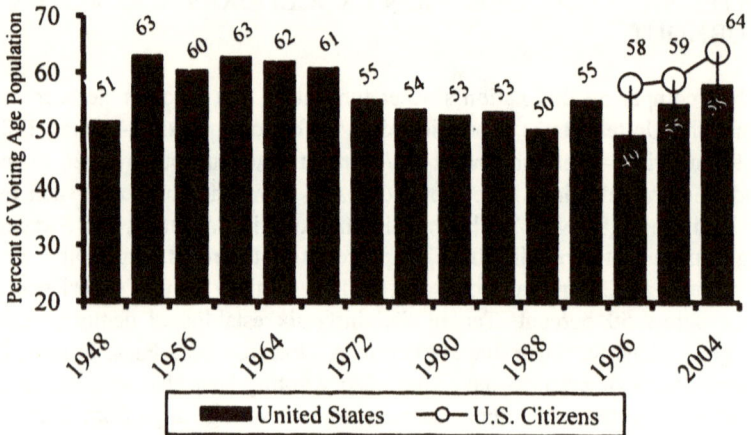

Source: Crocker, 1994; Federal Election Commission, 1996;
Election Services Inc., 1997; and U.S. Census, 2004.

Does the portrayal of voter turnout rates based on the voting-age citizenship population transform bleak U.S. voter turnout rates? In 2004 nearly two-thirds (64 percent) of the voting-age citizen population voted on Election Day, a 6-percentage-point difference from the reported voter turnout among the voting-age population (58 percent). In comparing the voter-turnout rates of voting-age citizens and the overall voting-age populations in the 1996 and the 2000 presidential elections, one finds a disparity of 9 percentage points and 4 percentage points, respectively. The magnitude or degree of voter turnout changes when using the voting-age citizen population as the common denominator. However, one does find that fewer people actually voted in the 1996 presidential election (105 million) compared to the 1992 election (114 million). On the other hand, the 2000 election, with 110 million voters casting a ballot, demonstrated a rise in voter-turnout figures compared to the 1996 election. The trend continued in 2004, with 125 million voters showing up at the polls on Election Day.

Whether one compares voter-turnout rates based on the citizen voting-age population or the actual voting-age population, one finds that voter turnout in the United States has experienced a steady increase since the 1992 presidential election, suggesting that voter registration and turnout reform measures such as the National Voter Registration Act may be the reason for increased voter turnout rates.

ELECTION-DAY TURNOUT IN ARIZONA

In comparing voter turnout in Arizona to the national rate, one finds a similar rise-and-drop trend up until the 1992 election. An average voter turnout gap of 10 percentage points existed between the nation and Arizona for the period 1952 to 1968; an 8-percentage-point difference between 1972 and 1980; and a 4-percentage-point difference between 1984 and 1996. After a citizen-initiated motor-voter program in 1983 and state-initiated voter-registration programs in 1992 were implemented in Arizona, the declining voter turnout rates reversed, and voting in Arizona began to climb, narrowing the Arizona–U.S. turnout gap. As exemplified in figure 1.2, Arizona's voter turnout climbed from 44 percent in 1980 to 46 percent in 1984 and 1988, and to 54 percent in 1992. In the 1992 presidential election more than one half of Arizonans (54 percent) went to the polls—the first modern election to captivate a majority of Arizona's voting population since the 1964 presidential election.

At first glance, voter turnout in the 1990s was encouraging. The 1992 presidential election demonstrated that American citizens' participation in voting significantly increased for Arizona as well as the nation as a whole, a practice that would hopefully pave the way for future elections.

It was presumed that state-initiated voter registration reforms may have contributed to the rise in the 1984, 1988, and 1992 presidential-election turnouts. Election reformers anticipated that once national-mandated NVRA procedures were implemented the surge in voter turnout would continue. However, the 1992 presidential election proved otherwise. Like national voter turnout (49 percent), Arizona's voter turnout plummeted in the 1996 presidential election, to 45 percent. The 1996 presi-

FIGURE 1.2
Arizona Acutal and Citizen Voter Turnout for Presidential
Elections: 1948-2004

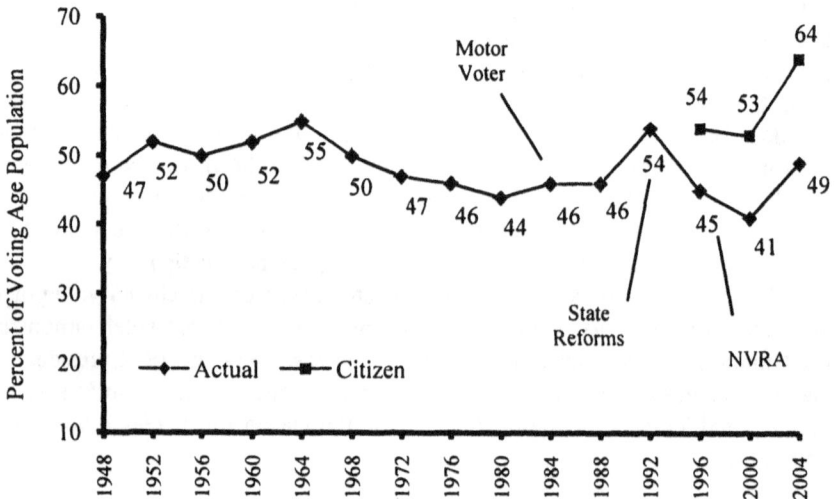

Source: Crocker, 1994; Election Data Services Inc., 1997; Bureau of the U.S. Census, 2000, 2004; and State of Arizona, 2000, 2004.

dential election-day turnout results were disappointing, marking the lowest rate, 48.9 percent nationally, in more than seventy-two years.[5] For Arizona, voter turnout in the 1996 presidential election reverted to prereform election years, where less than a majority of Arizonans voted. Arizona's voter turnout continued its downward trend in 2000 to an all-time low of 41 percent, rebounding somewhat in 2004.

Similar to national turnout rates, well over a majority of Arizona's voting-age citizen population made it to the polls on Election Day. For the 1996 presidential elections, 54 percent of Arizona's citizen population voted. Again, for the 2000 election, 53 percent turned out. The 2004 presidential election experienced the largest turnout in Arizona's election history, with 64 percent of the voting-age citizen population casting a ballot on Election Day—a 15-percentage-point difference from the reported voter turnout among the voting-age population (49 percent). Similar to U.S. voter turnout, the magnitude or degree of Arizona's voter turnout changes when using the voting-age citizen population as the common denominator.

The sharp decline in voter turnout in the 1996 and 2000 presidential elections raises suspicions about the value of government-initiated voter registration programs like the NVRA. The assumption that easing the costs associated with voting induces higher turnout rates becomes less significant than the assumption that individual socioeconomic characteristics influence an individual's level of political participation.

ARIZONA COMPARED TO OTHER WESTERN STATES

Arizona's average voter turnout rate is ranked among the bottom quartile of the eleven western states. As demonstrated in table 1.1, Arizona's median voter turnout for the previous ten presidential elections is ranked second to the last (47 percent). Arizona's voter turnout trails Montana, Utah, Oregon, and Idaho, which are positioned in the upper quartile, followed by Colorado, Washington, Wyoming, and New Mexico ranked in the median quartile. Along with Arizona in the lower quartile are California and Nevada.

For the 1968 and 1972 presidential elections, Arizona ranked last in voter turnout (50 percent and 48 percent, respectively), while Utah ranked first (77 percent and 69 percent, respectively) among the western states. For the next four presidential elections (1976, 1980, 1984, and 1988), Nevada's voter turnout dropped and recorded the lowest voter turnout (48 percent, 41 percent, 42 percent, and 42 percent, respectively), while the highest voter turnout was shared by Utah

TABLE 1.1

Voter Turnout and Average Turnout for Western States

Presidential Elections: 1948 to 2004

State	AZ	CO	CA	ID	MT	NM	NV	OR	UT	WA	WY
2004	48	62	47	59	63	54	48	67	56	61	63
2000	42	57	44	55	62	47	44	61	53	57	61
1996	45	53	43	58	63	47	39	58	50	55	60
1992	53	61	49	64	68	51	50	66	64	60	61
1988	46	56	47	58	62	49	44	57	61	53	52
1984	45	55	50	60	65	51	42	62	62	58	53
1980	45	56	49	68	65	51	41	62	65	58	53
1976	49	60	51	62	64	55	48	62	69	61	58
1972	48	60	60	63	68	58	51	62	69	64	64
1968	50	65	60	73	68	61	54	66	77	66	67
AVG	47%	59%	50%	62%	65%	52%	46%	62%	63%	59%	59%

Source: Statistical Abstract of the United States, 1972, 1976, 1980, 1987, 1992, 1996, 2001, 2004, 2006. The 1968 voting-age population is the resident population twenty-one years old and over. The 1972 voting-age population is the population eighteen years old and over.

with 69 percent in 1976, Idaho with 68 percent in 1980, and Montana with 65 percent in 1984 and 62 percent in 1988.

All western states reported a surge in voting for the 1992 presidential election; California reported the lowest voter turnout (49 percent), replacing Arizona (53 percent) and Nevada (50 percent). Consequently, for the 1996 election all western states reported a sharp decline in voter turnout with the exception of Wyoming. Utah and Nevada's voter turnout plunged by 14 and 11 percentage points, respectively. In addition, Nevada reported the lowest voter turnout, with 39 percent of the state's electorate making it to the polls.

In 2000, most western states reported a rise in voter turnout, with the exception of Arizona, Idaho, Montana, and New Mexico. Arizona reported the lowest voter turnout (42 percent) among the western states, while Montana had the highest with 62 percent. In 2004, all western states reported an increase in voter turnout. California was ranked eleventh, with 47 percent voter turnout, followed by Arizona and Nevada, with 48 percent voter turnout each.

THE ENFRANCHISED PUBLIC: WHO ARE THE VOTERS?

Surveys indicate that Americans who have a stake in society are much more likely to vote. In other words, individuals who are socially connected[6]—married, educated, employed, economically stable, older, have children, and own a home—are more likely to turn out and cast a vote.

Survey data presented in table 1.2 suggests that rates of voter turnout increasingly differ for individuals within specific demographic-based categories of income, education, age, racial/ethnicity, employment status, and tenure occupancy for the 1984, 1988, 1992, 1996, 2000, and 2004 presidential elections. Education is an essential socioeconomic characteristic associated with one's level of political participation. Education levels directly affect an individual's employment, occupation, and economic status within our society. "People with access to financial resources can use their resources to enhance their political voice"[7]; therefore, individuals with higher levels of education and income vote at significantly higher rates. Based on the last six presidential elections, on average, 75 percent of those with bachelors or professional degrees were more likely to vote, compared to 53 percent of those with a high school diploma and 33 percent of those with nine years of formal education or less.

Voting has decreased significantly for those individuals with nine years of education or less. In the 1984 presidential election more than two-fifths (43 percent) of those with nine years of formal education or less went to the polls, compared to 37 percent in 1988, 30 percent in 1996, and 27 percent in 2000. Only 23 percent of those with nine years of formal education or less voted in the 2004 presidential election. An individual's income level and employment status are closely related to his/her level of education. For the 2004 election, 73 percent of the voting electorate with annual family incomes of $50,000 or more reported voting in the election, whereas, only 36 percent of those with family incomes of less than $10,000 cast a ballot. Averaging the last six presidential elections, the electorate

TABLE 1.2 Voted in Presidential Elections: 1984 to 2004						
Demographic Characteristics	Percent Reported Voting of VAP					
	1984	1988	1992	1996	2000	2004
Race/Ethnicity						
White	61	59	64	60	56	60
African American	56	52	54	51	54	56
Latino	33	29	29	27	27	28
Age						
18-24	37	33	39	31	32	42
25-34	55	48	53	43	44	47
45-54	68	67	69	62	53	64
65-74	72	73	74	70	70	71
Education						
9 years or less	43	37	35	30	27	23
High School	59	55	58	49	49	49
College: 4 + years	77	75	80	73	72	74
Family Income						
$9,999 or less	43	39	37	33	32	36
$10,000 to 14,999	54	48	47	40	38	39
$15,000 to 24,999	59	55	59	46	43	*
$35,000 to 49,999	73	70	76	59	58	*
$50,000 and over	76	76	80	70	69	73
Gender						
Female	61	62	62	56	56	60
Male	59	60	60	53	53	56
Employment						
Employed	62	58	64	55	56	60
Unemployed	44	39	46	37	35	46
Tenure						
Owner	72	70	69	62	62	65
Renter	44	40	44	36	36	39

Source: U.S. Bureau of Census, 1983, 1989, 1993, 1998, 2002 and 2006.* For the 2004 Election, the U.S. Census created new categories for family income, the $15,000 to $24,999 and $35,000 to $49,999 categories are not similar, therefore voter turnout is not reported for the aforementioned income categories.

with family incomes of $50,000 or more were twice as likely to vote (74 per cent) as those with family incomes of $10,000 or less (37 percent). Employed individuals (59 percent) are more likely to vote than unemployed individuals (41 percent).

Voting is significantly higher among older adults than younger adults. Seven out of ten citizens between the ages of sixty-five and seventy-four went to the polls, whereas only four out of ten adults between the ages of eighteen and twenty-four voted in the 2004 presidential election. Voter turnout among the eighteen- to twenty-four cohort has climbed significantly in recent years—from 31 percent in 2000 to 32 percent in 2000 and 42 percent in 2004, a 10-percentage-point rise.

In comparing voter turnout among the different racial/ethnic groups, there are major disparities when it comes to casting a vote. For the 2004 presidential election, only 28 percent[8] of Latinos reported going to the polls, compared to 56 percent of African Americans and 60 percent of Whites, a turnout difference of 28 and 32 percentage points respectively. When averaging the last six presidential elections, Latinos were less likely to vote (29 percent), compared to African Americans (54 percent), and Whites (60 percent). However, if one separates the citizen population from the total U.S. resident population, the gap in voter turnout between Latinos, African Americans, and Whites narrows substantially (see chapter two).

Political scientists and sociologists Bernard Berelson, Sidney Verba, Norman Nie, Raymond Wolfinger, Steve Rosenstone, and Ruy Teixeira attribute high and low levels of voter participation to the socioeconomic and psychological characteristics of voters. While noted scholars Raymond Wolfinger, Steve Rosenstone, Bingham Powell, Walter Dean Burham, Robert Jackman, Frances Fox Piven, and Richard Cloward suggest that high and low levels of voter participation are the result of the legal-institutional structure of election laws.[9]

EXPLANATIONS OF LOW VOTER PARTICIPATION

Over the past decades the aforementioned scholars have empirically examined the causes of low voter participation and concluded that declining political participation can be explained by applying either the social-psychological and/or the legal-institutional schools of thought.

The social-psychological explanation suggests that an individual's psychological attitude and social characteristics influence an individual's level of political participation. Individuals become nonparticipants in American politics due to individual socioeconomic characteristics (lower levels of education and income) and their psychological attitudes or beliefs about government. Individuals become politically apathetic (passive) and perceive a lack of political efficacy (ineffectiveness),[10] thus causing them to disconnect from the political process.[11] The legal institutional structure explanation suggests that individuals are encumbered with voter registration procedures that place the burden of registering to vote on the individual and not on the political structure. These studies have examined the consequences of post-1960s voter registration laws on voter participation and conclude that there is a strong relationship between progressive/liberal registration laws and higher levels of voter turnout.

Raymond Wolfinger and Steven Rosenstone (1980) applied a multivariate analysis model using both 1972 U.S. Census Bureau data and state-registration laws. They estimated the effect of reformed registration laws on the 1972 presidential election to determine if liberalized registration laws would change voter turnout rates. They suggested that if all fifty states had "liberalized registration laws,"[12] voter turnout in the 1972 presidential election would have increased by an additional 12.2 million voters, or 9.1 percent. They concluded that registration deadlines and office hours were obstacles to turnout in the 1972 election.[13]

Glenn Mitchell and Christopher Wlezein's study (1989, 1995) replicated Wolfinger and Rosenstone's study, with slightly different results. Utilizing U.S. Census Bureau data, Mitchell and Wlezein examined the effect of registration laws on voter registration and turnout rates for presidential and midterm elections in 1972, 1978, 1980, and 1982.[14] They found that "fully liberalized registration laws"[15] would increase voter registration by 8.6 percent[16] and voter turnout by 7.6 percent,[17] a difference of 1.5 percent from Wolfinger and Rosenstone's findings on voter turnout. On a state-by-state analysis Mitchell and Wlezein estimated that eliminating Arizona's closing dates (7.4 percent) would have a more significant impact on voter registration rates than eliminating purging (6.7 percent) and extending hours (2.8 percent). Arizona's voter turnout rates would increase more so if closing dates were eliminated (7.5 percent) than by extending voting hours (4 percent) and eliminating the purging process (2.7 percent). Overall, Mitchell and Wlezein estimated that Arizona could possibly increase voter registration rates by 14.3 percent and voter turnout rates by 13.6 percent.[18]

Ruy Teixeira in *The Disappearing American Voter* (1992) deduced findings very similar to Mitchell and Wlezein's conclusions. Teixiera expanded his study to include the 1984 midterm election and the 1988 presidential election. Like Mitchell and Wlezein, Teixeira estimated that voter turnout would increase by 7.8 percent if all states would liberalize their registration laws.[19] Similar to Mitchell and Wlezein's state-by-state analysis, Ruy Teixeira concluded that electoral reform would have a more significant impact in Arizona than in most other states because Arizona has one of the most regressive sets of registration laws in the United States. Teixeira projected that if Arizona reformed its election laws, voter participation would increase by 13.7 percent.[20]

Staci Rhine (1993, 1995) applied a cross-sectional, time-series design utilizing state-level data for presidential and midterm elections over a twenty-year period (1972–1992). Her study analyzed the relationship between state registration laws[21] and voter turnout to determine which registration reforms would change voter turnout. Rhine's findings suggest that if all states had implemented same-day registration, an active motor-voter program, and mail-in registration in the 1988 election, voter turnout would have increased by 10 percent.[22] Rhine's findings suggest that same-day registration and motor-voter registration reforms are more likely to influence voter turnout rates than mail-in registration and eliminating the purging process.[23]

Rhine's study examined the impact of motor-voter registration on voter turnout in Arizona, Colorado, and Michigan. She found that motor-voter registration had a "positive and significant" effect on voter turnout. The potential effect is determined by the level of implementation, which ranges from no motor-voter program to a minimal motor-voter program to an active motor-voter program. Each level adds almost 1 percentage point to voter turnout rates. Rhine's examination of Arizona's voter turnout rates prior to[24] and after[25] the implementation of the motor-voter program found that Arizona experienced an increase in turnout. However, Rhine is hesitant to conclude that Arizona's voter turnout increase is "absolutely" attributed to Arizona's motor-voter program.[26]

Furthermore, Rhine's research refutes Wolfinger's, Rosenstone's, Teixeira's, Mitchell's, and Wlezein's conclusions that liberalized voter registration laws will increase voter turnout rates. By examining individual registration factors and voter turnout, Rhine found that reformed voter registration procedure (i.e., relaxing purging procedures, earlier closing dates, mail-in registration, library and post office registration, motor-voter registration, and deputy registrars) "is not associated with a greater likelihood of voting. Furthermore, the combination of mail, motor-voter, or same day registration does not increase the likelihood of voting."[27]

Stephen Knack (1996) replicated Rhine's methodology and examined the effect of motor-voter programs on voter turnout during the 1976–1992 periods. Like Rhine, Knack concluded that "active" motor-voter programs have "positive and significant" effects on voter registration (3.8 percent) and voter turnout (2.4 percent) over the duration of several elections.[28] In addition, Knack suggested that the impact of motor-voter registration and turnout would climax by the fifth election and "turn downward" thereafter.[29] His findings rejected the argument that individuals registering through motor-voter programs will not turn out to vote. Knack projects that almost one-half of the registrants will cast their ballots on election day.[30]

Daniel Franklin and Eric Grier (1997) utilized a multiple-regression model to examine the impact of motor-voter laws on registration and turnout in motor-voter and non-motor-voter states for the 1992 presidential election. Their findings estimate that motor-voter laws will have more impact on voter registration turnout (2.3 percent) than voter turnout (2 percent).[31] Franklin and Grier's projected effect on voter turnout is comparable to Knack's findings.

Research examining the effects of voter-registration laws on voter turnout strongly suggests that progressive/liberal registration laws could increase voter turnout anywhere from 7.6 to 14 percent.[32] In Arizona, reforming the voter-registration laws could possibly increase voter turnout by 13.6[33] and 14.3 percent.[34]

According to Wolfinger, Rosenstone, and Teixiera, liberalized registration laws should have the greatest impact among nonvoting populations such as the poor, raising their turnout rate anywhere from 8.4 percent to 12.1 percent; the less educated, increasing their turnout rate anywhere from 8.9 percent to 10.7

percent; the young, raising their turnout anywhere from 9.8 percent to 10.6 percent; and minorities,[35] increasing their turnout anywhere from 9.3 percent to 11.3 percent.

This researcher acknowledges the vast array of research suggesting that social-psychological characteristics and legal-institutional barriers combined to influence the rate of voter participation. However, the present research focuses specifically on the relationship between institutional electoral laws and voter participation.

THE IMPLICATIONS FOR NONVOTING

The institutional electoral structure of voter registration and election laws affects 1) the selection of federal, state, and local elected officials who in return determine policy outcomes, and 2) the initiative process, citizen's right to bring forward policy initiatives. Chosen representatives are more apt to respond to individuals who vote than to individuals who do not vote,[36] which suggests that the individual's and/or group's level of electoral participation determine the representatives' levels of responsiveness. Low levels of electoral participation among disenfranchised populations produce a less responsive government and fewer policies aimed at addressing their particular needs.

NOTES

1. Authors Kenneth Janda, Jeffery Berry, and Jerry Goldman describe conventional political participation as an individual's interest in political campaigns, if the individual tried to persuade others about vote choices, if the individual attended party meetings, and if the individual worked on a political campaign. See Kenneth Janda, Jeffery M. Berry, and Jerry Goldman, *The Challenge of Democracy* (New York: Houghton Mifflin Co., 2001), p. 129.

2. Kenneth Janda et al., *The Challenge of Democracy*, pp. 130–131.

3. International Institute for Democracy and Electoral Assistance, "Voter Turnout Since 1945," retrieved May 2007, http://www.idea.int/publications/, p.84.

4. Innocuous sanctions are informal practices. For example, nonvoters may have difficulty getting a public-sector job or a new passport.

5. The 1924 presidential election reported a 48.9 percent turnout rate. See Walter D. Burnham, "The Turnout Problem," in *Classic Readings in American Politics*, 2nd ed. (New York: St. Matin's Press, 1990), p. 136–137. See also Ruy Teixeira, *The Disappearing American Voter* (Washington, D.C.: The Brookings Institution, 1992), p. 9.

6. Ruy Teixeira, *The Disappearing American Voter*, p. 57. See also Raymond E. Wolfinger and Steven J. Rosenstone, *Who Votes?* (New Haven: Yale University Press, 1980), pp. 13–60; and Angus Campbell et al., *The American Voter* (Michigan: Univ. of Michigan Survey Research Center, 1964), pp. 250–265.

7. Edward D. Greenberg and Benjamin I. Page, *The Struggle for Democracy*, (New York: Addison Wesley Longman Inc., 1999), p. 139.

8. Latino voter turnout percentage includes citizens and noncitizens.

9. Frances Fox Piven and Richard A. Cloward, *Why Americans Don't Vote*, (New York: Pantheon Books, 1988), pp. 96–121.

10. Bernard R. Berelson, Paul F. Lazarsfeld, and William N. McPhee, *Voting*, (Illinois: University of Chicago Press, 1954), p. 34.

11. Ruy Teixeira, *The Disappearing American Voter*, p. 57.

12. In Wolfinger and Rosenstone's study, liberalized registration laws refer to eliminating the closing date, establishing regular office hours, adding evening and/or Saturday registration, and allowing absentee registration. See Raymond E. Wolfinger and Steven J. Rosenstone, *Who Votes?*, pp. 90–91.

13. Ibid., p. 91.

14. Mitchell and Wlezein's study used 1972, 1978, 1980, and 1982 census data. The census data was aggregated, and a 25 percent random sample was selected. See Glenn E. Mitchell and Christopher Wlezien, "The Impact of Legal Constraints on Voter Registration, Turnout, and the Composition of the American Electorate," *Political Behavior* (1995): p. 184.

15. In Mitchell and Wlezein's study, fully liberalized registration laws refer to the thorough liberalization of three laws: 1) the elimination of closing dates, 2) the elimination of periodic purges, and 3) extended voter registration hours. See Glenn E. Mitchell and Christopher Wlezien, "The Impact of Legal Constraints on Voter Registration, Turnout, and the Composition of the American Electorate," *Political Behavior* (1995): p. 184.

16. Ibid., p. 188.

17. Ibid., p. 191.

18. Ibid., p. 189.

19. In Teixeira's study, liberalization of registration laws refers to Election Day registration, universal evening and Saturday registration, universal regular office hours, and no purging. See Ruy Teixeira, *The Disappearing American Voter*, p. 111.

20. Ibid., p. 116.

21. Rhine's study examines the following voter registration laws: closing dates, mail-in registration, motor-voter registration, and the purge process. See Staci Rhine, "Registration Reform and Turnout in the American States," *American Politics Quarterly* (1995): pp. 419–421, and "Registration Reform and Its Relationship to turnout in the American States." Ph. D. dissertation (1993): p. 184.

22. Staci Rhine, "Registration Reform and Its Relationship to Turnout in the American States." Ph. D. dissertation (1993): p. 184.

23. Staci Rhine, "Registration reform and Turnout in the American States," *American Politics Quarterly* (1995): pp. 419–421.

24. The 1978, 1980, and 1982 elections.

25. The 1984, 1986, and 1988 elections.

26. Staci Rhine, "Registration Reform and its Relationship to Turnout in the American States." *Ph. D. Dissertation*, (1993): 83–88.

27. Ibid., p. 188.

28. Stephen Knack, "Does 'Motor Voter' Work? Evidence from State-Level Data," *The Journal of Politics* (1995): p. 806.

29. Ibid., p.806.

30. Ibid., p.808.

31. Daniel P. Franklin and Eric E. Grier, "Effects of Motor Voter Legislation." *American Politics Quarterly* (1997): pp. 110–111.

32. Steven J. Rosenstone and Raymond E. Wolfinger, "The Effect of Registration Laws on Voter Turnout," *The American Political Science Review* 72 (1978): pp. 32–36; Ruy Teixiera, *The Disappearing American Voter*, p. 114; Staci Rhine, "Registration Reform and Turnout in the American, *American Politics Quarterly* 23 (1995): pp. 419–421 and "Registration Reform and Its Relationship to Turnout in the American States." Ph. D. dissertation, 1993, p.184; and Glenn E. Mitchell and Christopher Wlezein, "The Impact of Legal Constraints on Voter Registration, Turnout, and the Composition of the American Electorate," *Political Behavior* (1995): pp. 118–191.

33. Ruy Teixiera, *The Disappearing American Voter*, p. 116.

34. Mitchell and Wlezein, The Impact of Legal Constraints on Voter Registration, Turnout, and the Composition of the American Electorate," pp. 189–190.

35. Previous research examining the impact of election reform on voter turnout specifically addresses the impact on African American registration and voter turnout.

36. Sidney Verba, Kay Lehman Schlozman, Henry Brady, and Norman Nie, "A Study of the Voluntary Activity of the American Public in Politics, Voluntary Associations, Charities, and Religion." *The Citizen Participation Project* (1989): p. 13.

CHAPTER TWO

LATINO POLITICAL PARTICIPATION

> We must arm ourselves, not with a rifle, but with the power of the vote.
> ⁓ Rudy Garcia, Community Organizer ⁓

Has "the Sleeping Giant"[1] awakened? Two presidential elections into the new millennium hailed record numbers of Latino voters. An estimated 5.9 million in 2000 and 7.5 million in 2004 swarmed to the balloting booths to cast their vote for presidential candidates.[2] In the nation's millenary elections,[3] the Latino share of the electorate grew from 5.4 percent for the 2000 presidential election to 6.0 percent for the 2004 presidential election.

The fact is that by the mid-21st century, one in four Americans will be of Latin heritage. Will the increasing number of Latinos translate into higher levels of political participation? In chapter two, I explore voter turnout among the Latino voting-age population (LVAP)[4] and the Latino voting-eligible population (LVEP).[5] While I focus on the Latino citizen population, I also analyze this group within the broader context of its potential growth and political clout.

As indicated in Chapter 1, low socioeconomic status indicators account for nonparticipation among American citizens. In this chapter, socioeconomic characteristics are examined to determine if the Latino population mirrors the general citizen population. Lastly, chapter two provides a brief but comprehensive survey of Latino political rights, beginning with the incorporation of Mexican citizens into the American political system. The treaty of Guadalupe Hidalgo became the starting point for formal relations between Mexican Americans, the largest Latino ethnic group, and the U.S. political system. The chapter concludes by describing the research setting—Arizona.

LATINO'S MILLENARY POPULATION

Seven years into the 21st Century, the United States population rose to 300 million people. The Latino population comprises 44.3 million or 15 percent of the total U.S. population, surpassing the size of the African American population (36.6 million) and representing the largest ethnic group in the United States.[6]

Figure 2.1 illustrates that since the 1970s the Latino population nearly quadrupled, from 9.5 million in 1970 to 35.3 million in 2000. Over the last three decades the Latino population increased each decade at a rate of 60 percent, 53 percent, and 55 percent, respectively. More amazing is the fact that each year between 2001 and 2006 the Latino population grew by more than 1.4 million, accounting for one-half of the U.S. population growth rate.[7] By 2030 the Latino population is projected to double (73.0 million), and by 2050 triple (102.5 million)

Figure 2.1: U.S. Latino Population: 1970 to 2050

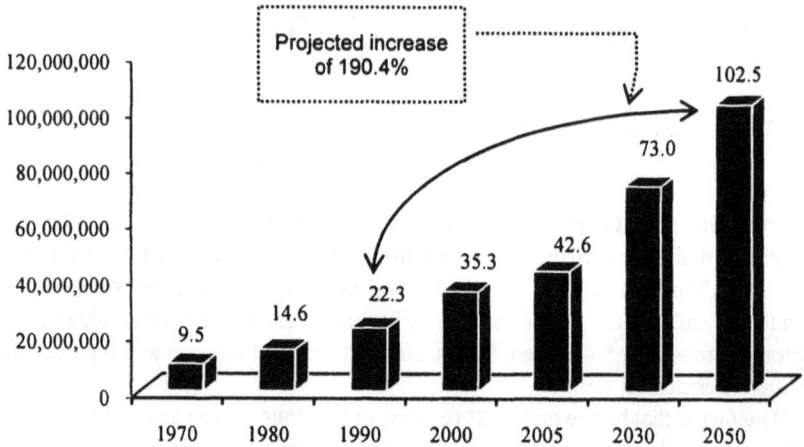

Sources: U.S. Census Bureau, "U.S. Interim Projections by Age, Sex, Race, and Hispanic Origin," March 18, 2004; "Historical Census Statistics on Population Totals By Race, 1790 to 1990," September 2002; and "Profiles of General Demographic Characteristics 2000," May 2001.

by 2050. These projections suggest that one-in-five individuals or 20 percent of the U.S. population will be of Latin descent by 2030.[8] By mid-century the Latino population will account for almost one-quarter (24.4 percent) of this nation's population. Much of the growth among the Latino population can be attributed to higher birth rates and massive immigration.[9]

The large, continuing arrival of Spanish-speaking immigrants creates both an advantageous and antagonistic political climate for American Latinos and Latinas. On the one hand the increase of Latin American immigrants will give rise to a potential Latino voting bloc that can influence decision-makers, and on the other hand it will produce an anti-Latino backlash against the Latino community. The only remedy is to assist new immigrants in gaining citizenship status, which is a prerequisite to acquiring one's right to vote. Will the increased numbers of Latinos translate into higher levels of political participation?

LATINO VOTER TURNOUT

When averaged, Latino voter turnout for presidential elections more than doubled over the last three decades, from 2.0 million in the 1970s[10] to 3.0 million in the 1980s[11] to 4.6 million in the 1990s.[12] The Latino share in election-day turnout increased from 2.43 percent in the 1970s to 3.0 percent in the 1980s to 4.2 percent in the 1990s. Similarly, the average number of Latino registered voters increased threefold, from 2.4 million in the 1970s[13] to 3.7 million in the 1980s,[14] 5.8 million in the 1990s,[15] and an estimated 8.4 million[16] for the millenary presidential elections.

Nationally, election-day turnout declined from 113.8 million in 1992 to 105 million in 1996 to110.8 million in 2000, and increased to 125.7 million for the 2004 presidential election[17] while, Latino voter turnout continued to grow, from 4.2 million in 1992 to 4.8 in 1996 to 5.9 million in 2000 to7.5 million for the 2004 presidential election.

Historically, Latino voter turnout has been lower than that of other racial/ethnic populations, notably White and African Americans (see Appendix B). In more recent elections Latino voter turnout has been comparable to Asian American voter turnout--significantly lower than White and African American voter turnout. With the exception of the 1984 presidential election, Latino voter turnout continuously declined, from 38 percent in the 1972 presidential election to an all-time low of 27 percent in the 1996 presidential election. For the 2000 and 2004 presidential elections, Latino voter turnout rose to 28 percent.

Over the last nine presidential elections Latino voter turnout averaged 30 percent, whereas African American voter turnout averaged 53 percent and White voter turnout averaged 61 percent. While the race gap between Whites and African Americans has narrowed to within 9 percentage points, it has widened for Latinos to 31 percentage points. The race gap between Latinos and African Americans has also increased, to 22 percentage points.

Latino voter turnout for presidential elections increases significantly when the noncitizen population is extracted from the Latino voting-age population base (see Appendix C). The disparity between Latino voter turnout and Latino citizen voter turnout averaged 17 percentage points over the last nine presidential elections. Latino citizen voter turnout wavered between a high of 48 percent and a low of 44 percent, with the exception of the 1972 presidential elections where more than a majority (55 percent) of Latino citizens voted. Latino citizen voter turnout averaged 47 percent between 1972 and 2004.

When the noncitizen population is omitted from the Latino voting-age population, the race gap between Latinos, Whites, and African American voting rates narrows substantially. In averaging voter turnout between 1972 and 2004, the voting disparity between Whites and Latinos narrowed to close to one-fifth more Whites casting a vote than Latinos (61 and 48 percent, respectively). The race gap is less evident between Latinos (48 percent) and African Americans (53 percent), an average difference of 5 percent over the last nine presidential elections.

LATINO POLITICAL CLOUT

Collectively, the Latino community has the potential to sway elections. In 2004, 82 percent of Latinos resided in eleven states,[18] which, when combined, comprise 212 of the 270 electoral votes needed to win the presidential election.[19] As the number of Latinos living in the United States rises, their potential to influence the electoral process increases, but only if the Latino population exercises their political clout.

Latino voter participation varies considerably from state to state (see Appendix D). In ten states, Latinos represent almost one-quarter (23.2 percent) of the total voting-age population, and one-sixth (16.5 percent) of the total citizen voting-age population. For the 2004 presidential election the Latino share of total voters in the ten states—New Mexico, California, Texas, Arizona, Nevada, Florida, Colorado, New York, New Jersey, and Illinois—was 8 percent of the individuals actually voting on election-day, ranging from a high of 33 percent in New Mexico to a low of 5 percent in Illinois.

New Mexico has the highest percentage of Latino residents, with 44 percent of New Mexicans being of Latin descent, followed by California and Texas, with 36 percent each, then Arizona with 29 percent, Nevada with 24 percent, Florida and Colorado with 20 percent each, New York and New Jersey tied with 16 percent, and lastly, Illinois with 15 percent. The Latino population makes up about one-quarter of the voting-age population in the eleven states, and roughly 17 percent of the Citizen voting-age population. The disparity between the Latino voting-age population and Latino citizen voting-age population varies from state to state. Almost one-half a of Nevada (49.8 percent), New Jersey (47.5 percent), Arizona (45.7 percent), and California (45.4 percent) voting-age Latinos are noncitizens; two-fifths of Florida (40.3 percent) and Illinois' Latino population (41 percent) are noncitizens; around one-third of New York (31.8 percent) and Colorado (37 percent) residents are noncitizens, compared to Texas (29.5 percent) and New Mexico with only 10.6 percent of its Latino voting-age population having noncitizenship status.

In the 2004 presidential election the Latino share of the electorate varied in the eleven states. New Mexican Latinos made up almost one-third (32.9 percent) of its state's electorate, followed by Texas (19.2 percent), California (16.2 percent), Arizona (13.2 percent), and Florida (11.1 percent).In the other states (Nevada, New York, Colorado, New Jersey, and Illinois), Latinos comprised less than 10 percent of their state's electorate. Still, the Latino electorate as a voting bloc comprises 13 percent of the total electorate in the eleven states, enough to sway an electoral outcome.

Many Latino community members are relatively new immigrants. Latinos and Latinas are a younger population group, have a smaller proportion of higher levels of formal education, and have a disproportionate number of individuals living in poverty. When combined, the socioeconomic characteristics may impede Latino political progress.

LATINO SOCIOECONOMIC CHARACTERISTICS

Over the last decade Latinos have experienced growth in various socioeconomic indicators, yet a disparity still exists between them and their White, African American, and Asian American counterparts (see Appendix E). When comparing median household income levels, Latinos earn significantly less than Whites and Asian Americans and slight more than African Americans and Native Americans.

In 2006 the median household income for Latinos was $37,781 compared to $52,423 for White households and $64,238 for Asian American households. Latino households earned slightly more than African American households ($31,969) and Native Americans households ($33,762). Keep in mind that Latino households are larger (3.62) than Asians (3.11), Native Americans (2.80), African Americans (2.74), and White (2.43) households. White and Asian per capita income—$30,431 and $30,474, respectively—is almost double that of Latinos and African Americans ($15,421 and $17,902) per capita income. Between 1999and 2006, Latinos and African Americans did see a modest increase in their per capita incomes ($3,800 and $3,500, respectively), whereas White and Asian American income increased by $6,322 and $9,340, respectively. The income gap between Latinos, African Americans, and Native Americans and their White and Asian American counterparts continues to widen, producing a recognizable wealth inequity.

In 2006, one in four White households and one in three Asian American households had incomes of $100,000 or more compared to Latino (12 percent) and African American households (13 percent). The majority of Latino (57.6 percent) and African American households (58.8 percent) have incomes of $50,000 or less. The number of Latino families living in poverty declined from 26 percent in 1998 to 21 percent in 2006.Yet more Latino families live in poverty than White families (8 percent) and Asian Americans families (10 percent). The poverty rate for African American families (24 percent) and Native Americans (27 percent) is significantly high.

While the gap between Whites and African Americans completing high school has narrowed, for Latinos it continues to widen. In 2003, a little over one-half (57 percent) of Latinos 25 years of age or older completed high school compared to Whites (89.4 percent), Asian Americans (87.6 percent), African Americans (80 percent), and Native Americans (73 percent) living outside tribal areas. Fewer Latinos (11 percent) receive college degrees than Whites (30 percent), Asian Americans (49.8 percent), African Americans (17.3 percent), and Native Americans (13 percent) living outside tribal areas.

The fact that the Latino population is younger than their non-Latino counterparts, and a larger percentage of their community is foreign-born, may account for some of the disparity in income levels and educational attainment. A little over one-third (33.7 percent) of the Latino population is 18 years of age or younger, compared to Asian Americans (22.8 percent), Whites (23.8 percent), African Americans (29.6 percent), and Native Americans (29.3 percent).The median age for Latinos is 27 years of age, compared to 39 years of age for Whites, 35 years of age for Asian Americans, 31 years of age for African Americans, and 30 years of age for Native Americans living outside tribal areas.

Significant sectors of the Latino community are foreign-born and are not U.S. citizens. In 2003, two in five Latinos (40.2 percent) were foreign-born, compared to 3.9 percent of Whites, 7.4 percent of African Americans, and 1.5 percent of Native Americans and Alaskan Natives. The Asian community has a sizeable foreign-born population (67.8 percent).However, Asians are three times (34.4 percent) more likely to become naturalized than Latinos (11.2 percent). Both Asian and Latino communities continue to have a substantial number of noncitizens in their communities (34.5 and 29 percent, respectively) The combination of socioeconomic conditions, foreign-born, noncitizenship status, language, and historical factors have systematically relegated fractions of the Latino community to a lower social, economic, and political tier, consequently contributing to the lower civic participation among Latino peoples.

The Latino political experience in the Southwest parallels the African American political experience in the South. In the past, Latinos and African Americans "encountered many legal and institutional barriers to full participation as citizens."[20] Formally, Mexican Americans were granted civil and political rights, yet in practice, barriers such as state-sanctioned segregation in schools and housing, Jim Crow practices, and job discrimination[21] excluded them from "the right to participate that citizens enjoyed."[22] Today, Mexican Americans have the right to participate in the election process once they gain citizenship. However, Mexican Americans continue to struggle for the opportunity to participate on an equal plane in an "unequal" system.[23]

LATINO SUFFRAGE

An examination of American history clearly demonstrates that suffrage was a right only extended to a select few—white, male property-owners—and denied to the many—non-property owners, women, African Americans, Native Americans, and Latinos.

In theory the U.S. Constitution, U.S. Treaties, and state constitutions grant the formal or legal right to vote to all its citizenry. However in practice the American political process operates under informal governmental procedures. Arbitrary practices systematically incorporated into the normal day-to-day operation of American political institutions "undercut" equality and discourage minorities from actively participating in the political system.[24]

For the most part, election laws and electorate eligibility as prescribed in the U.S. Constitution, Article I, Section 2 and 4[25] remain under the control of individual states, unless state election procedures violate the Federal Constitution. In such cases, the federal government or the courts must intervene to rectify subtle and not so subtle registration and voting obstacles, such as poll taxes, literacy tests, all-White primaries, acts of violence,[26] English-only elections, annual voter registration, and residency criteria, which impede minority citizens from actively participating in the political system.

The Fourteenth Amendment of 1868 secured U.S. citizenship for all individuals born in the United States, including Latinos, and prohibited states from "making or enforcing any law which shall abridge the privileges or immunities of citizens of the United States."[27] The Fifteenth Amendment of 1870 prohibited the federal government and states from denying citizens the right to vote based on "race, color or previous condition of servitude."[28] The

Nineteenth Amendment of 1920 granted women the right to vote[29], including Latino women. The Twenty-fourth Amendment of 1964 abolished the Poll tax.[30] The Twenty-sixth Amendment of 1971 granted 18 year olds the right to vote.[31] The Civil Rights Act of 1964 was enacted to safeguard the voting rights of minorities. The Voting Rights Act of 1965 was designed to protect the voting rights of African Americans against state-legislated impediments aimed at disenfranchising the African Americans. The Voting Rights Acts Amendments of 1970 prevented the dilution of minority votes through gerrymandered or at-large districts and extended the protection of voting rights for African Americans to 1975. The Voting Rights Act Amendments of 1975 extended voting rights protection for another 7 years, banned literacy tests nationally, and added protection of language-minority groups under the original Voting Rights Act. The 1982 Voting Rights Act Extension extended the protection of voting rights for an additional 25 years, the language minority provision for an additional 10 years, and included assistance for illiterate or handicapped people.[32] The 1992 Voting Rights Act extended the language minority provision for an additional 15 years.[33] In 2006, President George W. Bush reauthorized the Voting Rights Act for an additional 25 years.[34]

All of the Constitutional Amendments, Treaties, and Civil Rights Acts described were enacted to ensure the protection of the civil rights of minorities, but territorial, state, and municipal public officials circumvented the law to create registration and voting procedures that were applied unequally toward Mexican Americans. From the time that the United States acquired Mexican Territory and its population, there has been duplicity in the granting of rights and privileges.

The shadow of conquest—the Mexican American War of 1846— characterizes Mexican Americans' political power within the context of the American political system. The Treaty of Guadalupe Hidalgo of 1848 defined the relationship between the United States and its Mexican citizenry. Article VIII of the treaty legally granted American citizenship to "those who shall prefer to remain in the said territories, may either retain the title and rights of Mexican citizens, or acquire those of citizens of the United States,"[35] and Article X bestowed to the Mexican Americans "the enjoyment of all the rights of citizens of the United States according to the principles of the Constitution."[36] However, history clearly demonstrates that after the United States took possession of the newly acquired Southwestern territory, Mexican Americans were relegated to the position of second-class citizens,[37] and the rights of American citizenship guaranteed under the Constitution to the newly naturalized Mexican American citizens became the subject of much controversy. The treaty should have allowed Mexican citizens remaining in the territory the opportunity to become U.S. citizens, and with American citizenship full suffrage; yet the right of Mexican Americans to vote was not fully recognized until California in 1850, New Mexico and Arizona in 1912 were granted statehood.[38]

Prior to statehood, territorial legislatures defined suffrage under their state constitutions, and granted the franchise only to white, male citizens. In Texas, Mexican Americans were not considered white citizens by the court. In California, Mexican Americans classifications went from "Caucasian" to "Indian."[39] California suffrage was extended to "every white, male citizen of Mexico who shall have elected to become a citizen of the United States."[40] Framers of California's State Constitution included the statement "white, male citizen" to exclude Indians, Blacks, and any Mexican who "looked like Indians"[41] but in 1870 California's Supreme Court ruled in *People v. de la Guerra* "the admission of California as a state constituted the positive act that conferred citizenship on former Mexican nationals"[42] as well as the right to vote.

In New Mexico, only "free white male inhabitants residing within the limits of the United States" had the rights of citizenship. Before Mexican citizens were granted territorial citizenship, they had to "renounce allegiance to the Mexican Republic."[43] Since New Mexico was a territory and not a state, many of the Mexican American citizens' civil rights were limited.

> they were not allowed to vote for their governor or for the president of the United States; the decisions of their elected representatives were subject to federal approval; and they did not have an independent judiciary.[44]

The Organic Act of 1850 established Arizona as a territory and permitted the territorial legislature to decide on the right of suffrage:

> Every free white male inhabitant, above the age of twenty-one years, who shall have been a resident of said territory at the time of the passage of this act, shall be entitled to vote at the first election, and shall be eligible to any office within the said territory, but the qualifications of voters and of holding office at all subsequent elections, shall be such as prescribed by the legislative assembly: Provided, that the right of suffrage, and of holding office, shall be exercised only by citizens of the United States, including those recognized as citizens by the treaty with the Republic of Mexico.[45]

Arizona's Anglo politicians feared that "American influence will be swallowed up by the great preponderance of the Mexican vote."[46]

For Mexican Americans the early 1900s was a period when Mexican Americans "witnessed continual infringement upon their civil rights and abrupt as well as slight increase and decrease in their economic and social positions, even though numbers maintained an absolute increase."[47] Protecting Anglo influence was accomplished at the expense of disenfranchising Mexican American voters. Territorial legislatures enacted laws that placed conditions such as literacy tests and poll taxes on Mexican American voters.[48] In Arizona the literacy test "was intended, in part, to eliminate 'the ignorant Mexican vote,'" and voter registrars had considerable discretion in applying the law.[49] Once implemented, the number of Hispanic voters declined in several Arizona counties.[50] "Because of the decline in Hispanic voters in Cochise and Pima counties, nearly half of the precincts lacked enough voters to justify holding primary elections in 1912."[51]

The exclusion of Latinos from social, civil, and political process positioned them in a "subordinate ascriptive class."[52] According to Milton Gordon in *Assimilation in American Life* (1964), racial and ethnic groups encountered a range of assimilation strategies. Assimilationists strongly supported the notion that minority groups "must conform to the pre-existing Anglo-Protestant culture." Theories of assimilation (Acculturation/Anglo-conformity, cultural pluralism, and the melting pot) were applied to Mexican Americans. These theories were supposedly designed to integrate the Mexican American into mainstream culture. Mexican Americans were expected to discard their history, traditions, values, and language.[53] Not all racial and ethnic groups adapted to the dominant culture. Some groups, such as African Americans, Native Americans, and Latinos were not accepted and were excluded from participating in America's social, economic, and political institutions. As a result a more profound psychological barrier of exclusion for Latinos exists, which in part accounts for the disparity between White Americans and Mexican Americans in economic, social, and political status.

For many decades in the 20th century, Latinos were referred to by scholars as "forgotten people"[54] or "forgotten Americans"[55], which depict not only their political exclusion but also alienation from the mainstream of American life. Given such a prolonged state of legalized social and political exclusion, it is to be expected that even as legal barriers fade away there will be a time lag before Latinos achieve great political integration.

Ending state-mandated and bureaucratic impediments intended to disenfranchise the Mexican American population involved the labors of several Latino activists, political leaders, and community-based organizations. The Southwest Voter Registration and Education Project and the Mexican American Legal Defense and Education Fund (MALDEF) sought legal remedies for unequal treatment at the ballot box and initiated court challenges. After World War II, Mexican American political activism (primarily among military veterans) gave rise to numerous political organizations such as the Mexican American Political Association (MAPA) of California, the Political Association of Spanish-Speaking Organizations (PASSO) in Texas, and the American Coordinating Council on Political Education (ACCPE) in Arizona. Later the Chicano Movement of the 1960s created a political climate that gave rise to student and community-based organizations such as the Brown Berets, La Raza Unida, Los Siete de La Raza, Crusade for Justice, and the Movimiento Estudiantil Chicano de Aztlán (MECHA). The collective action of 1960s-style mass protest, coupled with established community-based organizations such as the GI Forum and League of United Latin American Citizens (LULAC), created an inclusive movement representing all facets of the Latino population.[56]

The amalgamation of Latinos, African Americans, and Native American coalitions of the 1960s and 1970s demanded fair and equal treatment for all minorities and forced the federal government to intercede and enact civil rights and voting rights laws such as the 24th Amendment (1964), which eliminated the poll tax in all federal elections.[57] The Voting Rights Acts (VRA) of 1965, 1970,

1975, 1982, 1992, and 2006 targeted "covered jurisdictions" in Alaska, Alabama, Arizona, Georgia, Louisiana, Mississippi, South Carolina, Texas, Virginia, and some counties in Connecticut, California, Colorado, Florida, Hawaii, Idaho, Massachusetts, Michigan, New Hampshire, New York, North Carolina, North Dakota, and Wyoming.[58] The VRA was aimed at states that had historically denied the franchise to African Americans and "language-minorities," which included Latinos, Asians, Native Americans, and Alaskan natives, even though it was intended as a temporary measure. Once racial and ethnic minorities integrated into the political process the VRA would no longer be necessary. However, a system that excluded these groups for decades could not be fixed in five years. The key provisions of the VRA:

1) prohibited any prerequisite voting procedure or practice, such as the literacy test and poll taxes in state and local elections that hindered the individual's right to cast his or her vote;

2) voting procedures were required to be precleared through the Department of Justice;

3) federally appointed "examiners" would be sent into the "covered jurisdictions" to "oversee" the voting process; and

4) extended "coverage" of the VRA to "language-minority." [59]

The Voting Rights Act seems to have eliminated the more blatant voting limitations confronting Latinos in the Southwest. Combined, reapportionment and the VRA increased the number of Latino elected officials in the Southwest. Since its inception, Latinos have utilized the VRA's special protections to challenge court electoral procedures that have violated their right to exercise their vote freely.[60]

Notwithstanding the progress achieved by the aforementioned laws, the present structure of election laws continues to be an obstacle to voting (e.g., closing dates, residency requirements, deputy registration systems, the purging process, etc.). These structural procedures discourage Latinos from becoming involved in the electoral system and are instrumental in disproportionately excluding them from the electoral process. Electoral reforms, such as motor-voter registration, mail-in registration, agency-based registration, and fail-safe provisions, were enacted to rectify past electoral practices of exclusion, thus producing a political system more widely accessible to a previously disenfranchised public.

For Latinos, especially those who are less educated, have limited English-speaking skills, and have incomes in the lower stratum of the socioeconomic ladder, the United States continues to operate under a façade of democratic principle. American institutions supposed to foster democratic participation among its citizenry have the opposite effect, that of denying political opportunities for Latinos. Rodney Hero's theoretical model of two-tiered pluralism describes the plight of the Latino political experience within the U.S. political system.

THE ENFRANCHISED LATINO: A PROFILE OF "LIKELY" AND "UNLIKELY" VOTERS

Reported voting rates among the different demographic groups indicate that socioeconomic factors are likely to influence turnout rates among the Latino voting community (see Appendix F). However, the magnitude of influence is less for the Latino voting community than the general voting community. In other words, the Latino voting community, with similar socioeconomic characteristics, is a quarter to one-half as likely to vote than the general voting community.

When examining reported voter turnout rates for Latinos by socioeconomic characteristics for the 1984, 1988, 1992, 1996, 2000, and 2004 presidential elections, one finds on average more than half (54 percent) of the Latino voting electorate with family incomes above $50,000, whereas one-fifth (20 percent) of those with incomes below $10,000 reported voting. Almost twice as many Latino college graduates (52 percent) went to the polls compared to high school graduates (28 percent).Only one in six Latinos with nine years or less of formal education went to the polls. Voting is much higher among older Latino populations than younger Latino populations. Almost half (48 percent) of Latino adults between the age of 65 and 74 reported voting, compared to only 17 percent of Latino adults between the age of 18 and 24, on average. Well over one-third (38 percent) of Latinos adults between the ages of 45 and 54 reported voting. On average more Latinas (31percent) than Latinos (27 percent) went to the polls in the last six presidential elections.

Even though Latino voting rates increase at each level of educational attainment, as family income rises and as Latinos mature they still lag behind the general voting community. Comparing educational attainment, three-fourths (75 percent) of the general electorate with college degrees went to the polls compared to 52 percent of Latinos holding college degrees between 1974 and 2004.Among families with reported incomes above $50,000, 74 percent of the general population went to the polls, compared with 54 percent of the Latino population with similar incomes. Over the last six presidential elections, more senior citizens in the general population (72 percent) than Latino senior citizens (48 percent) reported voting, and fewer Latino young adults (20 percent) than young adults in the general population (33 percent) reported voting. On average, more non-Latino females and males (60 and 57 percent, respectively) voted than Latino females and males (31 and 27 percent, respectively) in the last six presidential elections.

While nonvoters are found among all socioeconomic groupings, the Latino community is more likely than other racial communities to have a significantly higher number of nonvoters, which to an extent can be attributed to the disproportionate number of Latinos who possess many of the socioeconomic characteristics associated with lower voter turnout rates. As more and more Latinos progress in age, acquire higher educational levels, and increase their earnings, voter turnout rates will rise. However, socioeconomic characteristics alone do not completely explain the disparity among comparable levels of education, income, and age between Latinos and other ethnic groups.

THE LATINO POPULATION IN ARIZONA

In 2006, Arizona was home to an estimated 6.1 million people. Latinos make up 29 percent or 1.8 million of the state's residents, while Whites comprise 60 percent, or 3.6 million. The remaining 10 percent of Arizonians are divided among Native Americans (4 percent), African Americans (3.2 percent) and Asians (2.2 percent).[61]

Arizona experienced an estimated growth of 1.4 million people between 1990 and 2000, which ranked it as second among states in population growth.[62] During that same time period the Latino population just about doubled in size, exceeding 1 million.[63] Latinos accounted for well over two-fifths of Arizona's growth rate. More noteworthy is the fact that the number of Latino Arizonians grew by almost half-a- million (490,124) over the last six years (2000 to 2006).[64]

Figure 2.2 illustrates the general distribution of Latino residents in Arizona, from a low in Apache County to as high as 81 percent in Santa Cruz County. The vast majority of Arizona's Latinos reside in the mid-to southern parts of the state: Chochise, Pima, Maricopa, Pinal, La Paz, Yuma, Gila, Graham, Greenlee, and Santa Cruz counties. More than three-fourths reside in Maricopa and Pima counties.

In Maricopa County the majority of Latinos reside in Phoenix, accounting for around one out of four city residents. In Pima County most Latinos reside in Tucson, accounting for about a third of the city's residents. In 2000, three out of ten Latinos resided in the border counties of Cochise, Pima, Santa Cruz, and Yuma and accounted for a majority of the population in Santa Cruz and Yuma counties. Very few Latinos reside in the Northern counties of Mohave, Yavapai, Coconino, Navajo, and Apache.

FIGURE 2.2

Latino Population in Arizona Counties, 2000

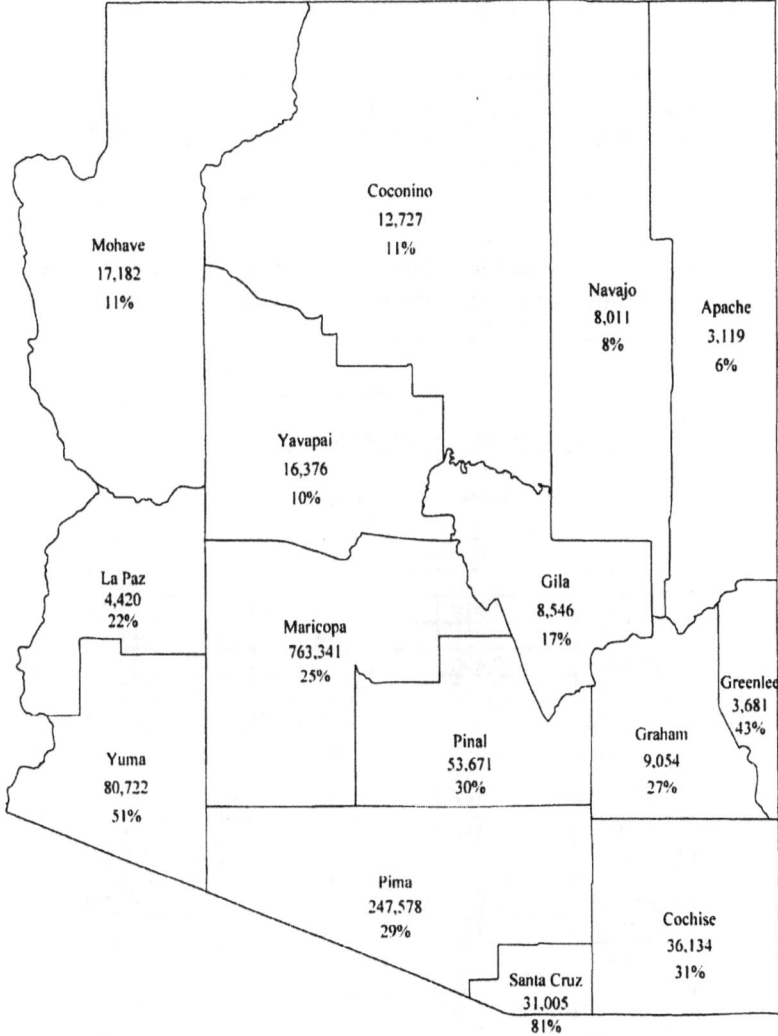

Source: U.S. Bureau of Census, Profiles of General Demographic Characteristics: 2002; and Map
Resources.

Table 2.1 illustrates county-level changes in Arizona's Latino population between 1990 and 2000.Mohave, Yavapai, and Maricopa counties recorded substantial growth in the number of Latinos. In Mohave County alone the Latino population more than tripled in size, from 4,919 in 1990 to 17,182 in 2000, the largest increase in the state of Arizona. In Yavapai and Maricopa counties the Latino population more than doubled in size. Much of the Latino population growth in Maricopa County occurred in the cities of Mesa, Glendale, Chandler, Phoenix city, and Scottsdale.

Other notable county-level increases in the Latino population growth occurred in Yuma (increased 86 percent), Pinal (increased 57.5 percent), and Pima (increased 51.6 percent) counties. In Pima County, two-thirds of the Latino population growth occurred in Tucson.

The largest growth in the Latino population occurred in the mid-state counties (increased 110.5 percent), followed by the northern counties (92.8 percent). In the border counties the Latino population increased 53.1 percent to 395,439, with the most significant increases occurring in Yuma (increased 80.8 percent) and Tucson city (increased 46.6 percent).

TABLE 2.1
County-Level Change in Latino Population

Counties	Latino Population in 1990	Latino Population in 2000	Change since 1990	Percent Change
Northern Counties				
Apache	2,599	3,119	520	20.0
Mohave	4,919	17,182	12,263	249.2
Yavapai	6,899	16,376	9,477	137.3
Coconino	9,696	12,727	3,031	31.2
Navajo	5,652	8,011	2,359	41.7
Total	29,765	57,415	27,650	92.8
Mid-State Counties				
Pinal	34,062	53,671	19,609	57.5
Gila	7,486	8,546	1,060	14.1
Greenlee	3,456	3,681	225	6.5
Graham	6,682	9,054	2,372	35.4
Maricopa	345,498	763,341	417,843	120.9
La Paz	3,139	4,420	1,281	40.8
Total	400,323	842,713	442,390	110.5
Border Counties				
Pima	163,262	247,578	84,316	51.6
Santa	23,221	31,005	7,784	33.5
Cochise	28,379	36,134	7,755	27.0
Yuma	43,388	80,722	37,334	86.0
Total	258,250	395,439	137,189	53.1

Source: Arizona State Data Center, "1990 Census of Population and Housing," 1990; and U.S. Bureau of Census, 2001.

LATINO POLITICAL PARTICIPATION IN ARIZONA

Given the objective of the National Voter Registration Act, one expects to find an increase in the number of Latino registrants. Figure 2.3 suggests that Latino voter registration and voting rates in Arizona's presidential elections for the 1980s, 1990s, and into the new millennium fluctuated from presidential election to presidential election. For the 1984, 1988, and 1992 presidential elections, Latino voter registration climbed from 36 percent to 40 percent to 45 percent, returning to the 1980 presidential election voter registration figures whereby over two-fifths of Arizona's Latino community registered to vote. For the 1996, 2000, and 2004 presidential elections, Latino voter registration averaged 32 percent, a drop of 13 percentage points from the 1992 election. Latino voter registration declined to an all-time low of 31 percent in the 2004 presidential election. Figure 2.3 illustrates that Latino voting rates climbed continuously from the 1980 presidential election to the 1992 presidential election—an increase of seven percentage points. However, in the 1996 presidential election Latino voting rates radically dropped. The 2000 presidential election brought 27 percent of Arizona's Latino community to the polls, an increase of 4 percentage points from the previous election. Again, in 2004 Latino voter turnout slightly dropped, to 26 percent.

FIGURE 2.3
Arizona Latino Voter Registration and Turnout in
Presidential Elections: 1982-2004

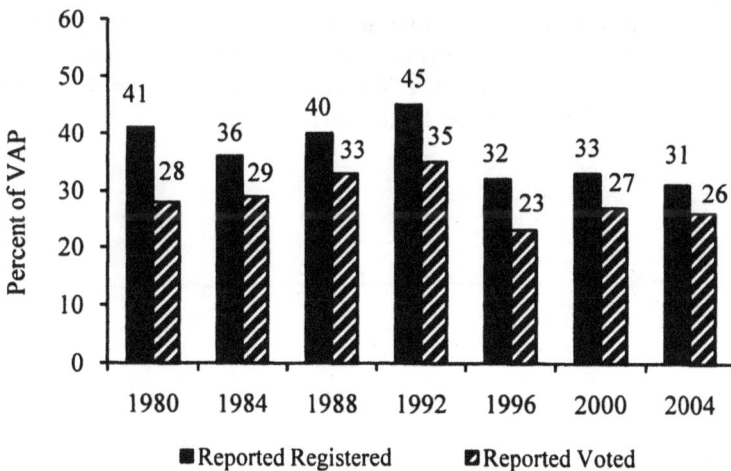

Source: The Hispanic Policy Development Project, 1984; U.S. Bureau of Census, Current Population Reports, 1985, 1989, 1993, 1998, 2002, and 2006.

ELIMINATING LEGAL-INSTITUTIONAL AND SITUATIONAL BARRIERS

In 2004, Latinos comprised 28 percent of the states' potential voters, a significant portion of the population that could swing a presidential election if they are 1) native or naturalized citizens, 2) registered to vote, and 3) vote on election day. Arizona's Latino voting-age population increased from 442,000 in 1992 to well over one million in 2004 (see Appendix G). For the 1992 presidential election, close to three-fourths of voting-age Latinos were U.S. citizens and eligible to vote; whereas in 2004 the Latino citizen voting-age population dropped to 54 percent, and the Latino noncitizen population rose to almost half a million. As Latinos joined the ranks of Arizona's eligible voters, roughly half were registered to vote in 2000 and 2004.Once registered to vote, eight in ten Latinos went to the polls on election day in 2000 and 2004.

The percentage of Latino noncitizens among Arizona's Latino population is a factor contributing to low Latino electoral participation. Yet the high numbers of Latino registered voters casting ballots on elections day does suggest that other factors, such as noncitizenship status and lack of political skills limit Latinos from participating fully in the electoral process. When legal-institutional barriers, such as literacy tests, poll taxes, and English-only voter registration material were removed, Latino participation levels increased. So one can presume that as additional legal-institutional barriers[65] and situational barriers[66] are eliminated, Latino political participation rates should continue to rise. Embarking on an evaluation of Arizona's state-initiated and federally-mandated NVRA provides an opportunity to examine empirical evidence measuring the relationship between electoral practices and the rate of participation among various demographic populations.

In the next chapter we journey into the political process encountered by the many political actors who have participated in the movement to reform Arizona's voter registration and election laws. The chapter sheds light on the politics of complying with the National Voter Registration Act.

NOTES

1. Latino scholars viewed the 1980s as the "Decade of the Hispanic." The "Sleeping Giant" was an analogy applied to the Hispanic population.
2..The Federal Election Commission officially reported 105,396,641 persons voted in the 2000 presidential general election. See "2000 official Presidential General Election Results," *Federal Election Commission on the Web*, (20 June 2001), http://fecweb1.fec.gov/pubrec/2000presgeresults.htm; U.S. Bureau of Census, "Voting and Registration in the Election of November 2000," *Current Population Reports*, Series P20-542 (Washington D.C.: U.S. Government Printing Office, 2002, pp. 5; U.S. Bureau of Census, "Reported Voting and Registration, by Race, Hispanic Origin, Sex, and Age, for the United States: November 2004," U.S. Census on the Web, (March 25, 2005).
3. A millenary election is referring to the 2000 and 2004 Presidential Election.
4. Latino voting-age population (LVAP) includes all individuals 18 years-of-age and older.
5. Latino voting-eligible population (LVEP) excludes the noncitizen population.
6. U.S. Bureau of the Census, "Profiles of General Demographic Characteristics 2000," *U.S. Census on the Web*, (May 2001) http://www.census.gov/prod/cen2000/index/html.
7. U.S. Census of the Bureau, "Annual Estimates of the Population by Sex, Race, and Hispanic or Latino Origin for the United States: April 1, 2000 to July 1, 2006," *U.S. Census on the Web*, (May 17, 2007), http://www.census.gov/ipc/www/usinterimproj/.
8. U.S. Bureau of the Census, "U.S. Interim Projections by Age, Sex, Race, and Hispanic Origin," March 18, 2004.
9. "We the Americans...Hispanics," *U.S. Department of Commerce*, pp 6-7. See also, "Census Figures Show Dramatic Growth in Asian, Hispanic Populations," *CNN on the Web* (30 August 2000), http://www. cnn.com/2000/US/08/30/ minority. population. html.
10. The 1972 presidential election was the first election the U.S. Bureau of the Census reported registration and voting data on the Spanish-origin population. For the 1972 presidential election, the U.S. Census reported 85,766,000 individuals voted of which 2,103,000 were of Spanish-origin heritage. For the 1976 presidential election, 86, 698,000 individuals voted of which 2,098,000 were of Spanish origin. See U.S. Bureau of the Census, "Voting and Registration in the Election of November 1972," Current Populations Report, http://www.census.gov/population/www/socdemo/voting/p20-253.html; and "Voting and Registration in the Election of November 1976," Current Populations Report, http://www.census.gov/population /www/ socdemo/ voting/ p20-322.html.
11. For the 1980 presidential election, the U.S. Census reported 93,066,000 individuals voted of which 2,453,000 were of Spanish origin. For the 1984 presidential election, the U.S. Census reported 101,878,000 individuals voted of

which 3,092,000 were of Spanish origin; and for the 1988 presidential election, the U.S. Census reported 102,224,000 individuals voted of which 3,710,000 were Hispanic. See U.S. Bureau of the Census, "Voting and Registration in the Election of November 1980, Current Populations Report, http:// www.census. gov/population/www/socdemo/voting/ p20-370.html; and "Voting and Registration in the Election of November 1984," Current Populations Report, http://www.census.gov/population/www/socdemo/ voting/p20-405.html; and "Voting and Registration in the Election of November 1988, Current Populations Report, http://www.census.gov/ population/www/ socdemo/voting/ p20-440.html.

12. Nationally, 113,866,000 individuals reported voting and 4,238,000 Hispanics reported voting in the 1992 presidential election. For the 1996 presidential election, the U.S. Census reported 102,224,000 individuals voted of which 3,710,000 were Hispanic See U.S. Bureau of the Census, "Voting and Registration in the Election of November 1992," *Current Population Reports*, Series P20-466 (Washington D.C.: U.S. Government Printing Office, 1993), pp. 4-5, and "Voting and Registration in the Election of November 1996," Current Populations Report, http://www.census.gov/population/www/socdemo/voting/ p20-504.html.

13. U.S. Bureau of the Census reported 2,495,000 registered Spanish-origin individuals for the 1972 presidential election. For the 1976 presidential election, 2,494,000 registered individuals were of Spanish origin. See U.S. Bureau of the Census, "Voting and Registration in the Election of November 1972," Current Populations Report, http://www.census.gov/population/www/socdemo/voting/ p20-253.html; and "Voting and Registration in the Election of November 1976," Current Populations Report, http://www.census.gov/population /www/ socdemo/ voting/ p20-322.html. Also, "Special Studies: Voting and Registration Highlights From the Current Population Survey: 1964 to 1980," *Current Population Reports*, pp. 5-6.

14. For the 1980 presidential election, the U.S. Census reported 2,984,000 registered individuals of Spanish origin. For the 1984 presidential election, the U.S. Census reported 3,794,000 registered individuals of Spanish origin; and for the 1988 presidential election, the U.S. Census began using the term "Hispanic," for individuals of Spanish heritage, and reported 4,573,000 registered Hispanics. See U.S. Bureau of the Census, "Voting and Registration in the Election of November 1980, Current Populations Report, http:// www.census. gov/ population/www/socdemo/voting/ p20-370.html; "Voting and Registration in the Election of November 1984," Current Populations Report, http://www.census. gov/population/www/socdemo/voting/p20-405.html; and "Voting and Registration in the Election of November 1988, Current Populations Report, http://www.census.gov/ population/www/ socdemo/voting/ p20-440.html.

15. Nationally, 5,137,000 Hispanics were reported registered the 1992 presidential election, and for the 1996 presidential election, the U.S. Census reported

6,573,000 Hispanics registered. See U.S. Bureau of the Census, "Voting and Registration in the Election of November 1992," *Current Population Reports*, Series P20-466 (Washington D.C.: U.S. Government Printing Office, 1993), pp. 4-5, and "Voting and Registration in the Election of November 1996," Current Populations Report, http://www.census.gov/ population/www/socdemo/voting/ p20-504.html

16. For the 2000 presidential election, the U.S. Census reported 7,546,000 Hispanics registered. For the 2004 presidential election, the U.S. Census reported 9,308,000 Hispanics registered. U.S. Bureau of the Census, "Voting and Registration in the Election of November 2000 (P20-542)." Current Population Report, http://www.census.gov/population /www/socdemo /voting/p20-542.html; and "Reported Voting and Registration, by Race, Hispanic Origin, Sex, and Age, for the United States: November 2004." Current Populations Reports, http://www.census.gov/population/www/socdemo/ voting/cps2004.html.

17. U.S. Bureau of the Census, "Voting and Registration in the Election of November 1992," *Current Population Reports,*Series P20-466 (Washington D.C.: U.S. Government Printing Office, 1993), pp. 4-5; "Voting and Registration in the Election of November 1996," *Current Population Reports*, Series P20-504 (Washington D.C.: U.S. Government Printing Office, 1998), pp. 3-4; "Voting and Registration in the Election of November 2000," *Current Population Reports*, Series P20-542 (Washington D.C.: U.S. Government Printing Office, 2002), p. 6; and "Voting and Registration in the Election of November 2004," *Current Population Reports,* Series P20-556 (Washington D.C.: U.S. Government Printing Office, 2005), p. 4.

18. "Estimates of the Population by Race and Hispanic or Latino Origin for the United States and States: July 1, 2006," *U.S. Census on the Web* (May 17, 2007).

19. Harold W. Stanley and Richard G. Niemi, *Vital Statistics on American Politics 1999-2000*, (Washington, D.C.: Congressional Quarterly, 2000), pp. 32-33.

20. Sidney Verba, Kay Lehman Schlozman and Henry E. Brady, *Voice and Equality* (Massachusetts: Harvard University Press, 1995), p. 229.

21. Chandler Davidson, *Minority Vote Dilution,* (Washington, D.C.: Howard University Press, 1989), p. 13.

22. Sidney Verba, Kay Lehman Schlozman and Henry E. Brady, *Voice and Equality* (Massachusetts: Harvard University Press, 1995), p. 229.

23. Ibid., pp. 511-513.

24. Rodney E. Hero, *Latinos and the U.S. Political System*, p. 189.

25. Article I, Section 2 of the United States Constitution states "The House of Representatives shall be composed of Members chosen every second Year by the People of the several States..."; and Section 4 of the United States Constitution states "The Times, Places and Manner of holding Elections for Senators and Representatives, shall be prescribes in each state by the Legislature thereof ;..."

See Angela Roddey Holder and John Thomas Roddey Holder, *The Meaning of the Constitution,* (New York: Barron's Educational Services, Inc.), pp 22-23.

26. See Hanes Walton, Jr. and Robert C. Smith, *American Politics and the African American Quest for Universal Freedom,* (New York: Addison Wesley Longman, Inc., 2000), pp. 160-164; and M. Margaret Conway, *Political Participation in the United States,* (Washington D.C: Congressional Quarterly, 1991), pp. 103-107.

27. Angela Roddey Holder and John Thomas Roddey Holder, *The Meaning of the Constitution,* (New York: Barron's Educational Services, Inc.), p. 91.

28. Ibid., p. 99.

29. Ibid., p. 104.

30. Ibid., p. 110.

31. Ibid., p. 113.

32. A brief description of the Constitutional Amendments and Voting Rights legislation was provided in "Voter Registration Reform: Pros & Cons," in *Congressional Digest,* (Washington   D.C: U.S. Government Printing Office, 1993), pp. 68-69. See also Chandler Davidson, *Minority Vote Dilution,* pp. 145-161.

33. "The Language Minority Provisions of the Voting Rights Act," *U.S. Department of Justice Civil Rights Division Voting Section on the WEB,* (11 February 2000), http://www.usdoj.gov/crt/voting/sec_203/activ_203.htm.

34. Mistique Cano, "Civil Rights Coalition Celebrates Renewal of Landmark Voting Rights Act," on the www.renewthevra.org (July 27, 2006).

35. Richard Griswold Del Castillo, *The Treaty of Guadalupe Hidalgo: A Legacy of Conflict,* (Oklahoma: University of Oklahoma Press, 1990), p. 189.

36. Ibid., p. 190.

37. David J. Weber, *Foreigners in their Native Land,* (Albuquerque, N.M.: University of New Mexico Press, 1973), p. 143.

38. Richard Griswold Del Castillo, *The Treaty of Guadalupe Hidalgo: A Legacy of Conflict,* pp. 66; 70.

39. Joel Spring, *Deculturalization and the Struggle for Equality,* (New York: McGraw-Hill, Inc., 2001), pp. 72-73.

40. Richard Griswold Del Castillo, *The Treaty of Guadalupe Hidalgo: A Legacy of Conflict,* p. 66.

41. Ibid., p. 66.

42. Ibid., p. 69.

43. Ibid., p. 70.

44. Ibid., p. 70.

45. Holmes, p. 51.

46. David J. Weber, *Foreigners in their Native Land,* p. 144.

47. Juan Gómez-Quiñones, *Roots of Chicano Politics, 1600-1940,* (Albuquerque, N.M.: University of New Mexico Press, 1994), p. 352.

48. See David R. Berman, *Reformers, Corporations, and the Electorate,* (Colorado: University Press of Colorado, 1992), p. 54; and Juan Gómez-Quiñones, *Roots of Chicano Politics, 1600-1940,* p. 352.
49. David R. Berman, *Reformers, Corporations, and the Electorate,* p. 92.
50. Ibid. [The same page as the preceding note]
51. Ibid. [The same page as the preceding note]
52. Mario Barrera, *Race and Class in the Southwest,* (Notre Dame: University of Notre Dame, 1979) p. 218.
53. Joe R Feagin and Clairece Booher Feagin, *Racial and Ethnic Relations,* (New Jersey: Prentice Hall, 1996) pp. 36-37.
54. George I. Sanchez, *Forgotten People,* (New Mexico: Calvin Horn Publisher, Inc., 1967) p. 98.
55. Julian Samora, ed., *La Raza: Forgotten Americans,* (Notre Dame: University of Notre Dame Press, 1966) pp. 201-211.
56. See Juan Gonzalez, *Harvest of Empire: A History of Latinos in America,* (New York: Penguin Books, 2000), pp. 177-182; and Juan Gómez-Quiñones, *Chicano Politics, Reality & Promise 1940-1990,* (Albuquerque, N.M.: University of New Mexico Press, 1990), pp. 34-36.
57. Chandler Davidson, "The Voting Rights Act: A Brief History," in Bernard Gofman and Chandler Davidson, eds. *Controversies in Minority Voting,* (Washington, D.C.: The Brookings Institution, 1992), p. 20.
58. Charles L. Cotrell, "Assessing the Effects of the U.S. Voting Rights Act: Introduction," *Publius* 16, no.4 (Fall 1986), p. 8.
59. For a more thorough discussion on VRA see Chandler Davidson and Bernard Gofman, eds. *Controversies in Minority Voting,* (Washington, D.C.: The Brookings Institution, 1992) pp. 7-85; and Charles L. Cotrell, eds. "Assessing the Effects of the U.S. Voting Rights Act," *Publius* 16, no.4 (Fall 1986), pp. 1-155.
60. John A. Garcia, "The Voting Rights Act and Hispanic Political Representation in the Southwest," *Publius* 16, no.4 (Fall 1986), p. 66.
61. U.S. Bureau of Census, "Estimates of the Population by Race and Hispanics or Latino Origin for the Unites States and States: July 1, 2006," *U.S. Census on the Web* (May 17, 2007).
62. U.S. Census Bureau, "States Ranked by Percent Population Change: 1990 to 2000," (April 2, 2001).
63. Arizona's Latino population grew from 688,353 in 1990 to 1,295,617 in 2000. Between 1980 and 1990, See U.S. Bureau of Census, "States Ranked by Hispanic Population in 1998," *U.S. Census on the Web* (15 September 1999).
64. U.S. Bureau of Census, "Annual Estimates of the Population by Sex, Race and Hispanics or Latino Origin for Arizona: April, 1, 2000 to July 1, 2006," *U.S. Census on the Web* (May 17, 2007).
65. Legal-institutional barriers, such as closing dates, residency requirements, deputy registration systems and the purging process.

66. Situational barriers consist of, but not limited to noncitizenship status, English-speaking skills, and political skills.

CHAPTER THREE

THE STRUGGLE TO REFORM ELECTION LAW IN ARIZONA

The battle is joined. But a national effort will be necessary before our democratic rhetoric matches our electoral reality. We can lay no claim to being a truly democratic nation until our elections reflect the will of all the people.

—Piven and Cloward—

The National Voter Registration Act, a comprehensive voter registration package, contained a motor-voter registration procedure that required driver's license employees to incorporate registering clientele into their daily routine, allowed for mail-in registration, provided for public agency–based registration, and forbade states from nonvoting purges. In addition it required each state to implement fail-safe voting procedures.

As of 1992, Arizona had implemented three of the five measures mandated by the federal government. Arizona had to fine-tune their motor-voter registration program to comply with the NVRA. The NVRA required Arizona to move from a passive system, "having the forms sitting on a countertop collecting dust," to a more active system where "the staff person actually offered the person assistance in completion of it [voter-registration form] and then collected and forwarded the completed forms."[1] Also, Arizona needed to put into operation public agency–based registration and fail-safe voting procedures. The success of the NVRA rested on the support and cooperation of intergovernmental agencies, public officials, and public organizations collaborating to develop operational procedures for the implementation of the NVRA by January of 1995.

THE IMPACT OF REFORMS ON THE MINORITY COMMUNITY

Arizona is one of nine states that require preclearance of election-law changes by the Justice Department because of past violations of Civil Rights laws.[2] Arizona is considered a "covered jurisdiction" under the special provisions of the Voting Rights Act of 1965. The Voting Rights Act of 1965 and the 1970, 1975, 1982, and 1992 amendments safeguard the voting rights of minority populations. The act prohibits "tests or devices" that previously were used to discriminate against minorities, such as literacy tests, education requirements, and English-only elections and procedures.[3] The special provision applies to states that have demonstrated a history of "employing discriminatory tests, devices, or practices in voting." Under the special-provision clause, Arizona must submit election-law changes to the Attorney General for clearance. The purpose of the special provision clause is to assure accessibility to the election process and assure that election practices do not discriminate against minority voters.[4]

In areas where minority populations represent 5 percent of the population, Arizona is required to provide bilingual election material and assistance. Under the bilingual provision, Arizona must "provide written translations in Spanish, and oral assistance for Navajo, Hopi, and Havasupi Indians."[5]

The Navajo language traditionally is an oral language. Mail-in registration could discriminate against those "unable to read, write, and/or speak English, and might encourage nonminority voting at the expense of minority voting, thereby diluting minority electoral power.[6] By not providing bilingual election material to the voters, language minorities have "less opportunity than other American citizens to participate effectively in all phases of the political system."[7]

Following precedents, if mail-in registration material and procedures are not bilingual then the administration of the mail-in registration process might be considered an exclusionary practice that discriminates against minorities by silencing their voices, therefore diluting their voting power. On the one hand, if the legislation were administered effectively, for example creating "a comprehensive, coordinated bilingual election program assuring [minority] populations equal access to all phases of the electoral process,"[8] it would increase minority participation, thus strengthening minority voting power.

MOVING TOWARD REFORM

The struggle to reform Arizona's election laws evolved over a span of two decades, the 1980s and 1990s, and involved many political actors working simultaneously within the state's political system. Several key developments included the 1982 motor-voter citizen initiative, the 1988 recall movement against Arizona governor Evan Mecham for misusing funds,[9] and a 1988 lawsuit against Arizona's Navajo and Apache counties for not providing bilingual election materials.[10] Further, the 1990 "AzScam" investigation into illegal campaign contributions and bribery,[11] citizen complaints, and a 1990 election recount produced a special panel to review Maricopa's voter registration and election procedures.[12] The result was a renewed interest in local politics—"more people made up their minds to become participants in this democracy."[13] These developments created a political climate that demanded Arizona's government officials to act. The reforms to "liberalize" Arizona's voter registration and election laws came in the form of legislative referendums and state- and county-initiated election programs. Before the election-reform movement, "Arizonans faced so many barriers to the ballot that it's a wonder anyone gets registered, let alone votes."[14] After the election-reform movement, Arizona was "further ahead" in election reform than other states.[15]

Arizona's Political Actors Take Action

After the 1988 presidential election, Phoenix Union High School Board incumbent Mary Carr asked for a recount after it was discovered that 273 votes for the incumbent went to another candidate in the Phoenix Union High School District election. After a lawsuit was filed alleging improper voter-registration and election procedures, the Maricopa County Board of Supervisors created an Elections Oversight Committee to review the Election Department of the County Recorder's office to identify weaknesses in its operating procedures.[16]

That same year, the U.S. Department of Justice filed a lawsuit against the state of Arizona and Apache and Navajo Counties. According to the lawsuit, state and county election officials were in violation of the Voting Rights Act of 1965 because election officials had failed to provide bilingual ballots and election materials, thereby infringing on the voting rights of Navajo Indians.[17]

Discrepancies surrounding the handling of election procedures in the 1988 presidential election led to two citizen-initiated drives to change Arizona's election laws. In 1989, Ed Buck, a Phoenix businessman, initiated a petition drive that would open primaries to all registered voters and allow for election-day registration. If enough signatures were gathered, both measures would be placed on the 1990 general-election ballot. Buck had been successful in gathering more than 300,000 registered-voter signatures toward the recall effort of Governor Mecham in 1988.[18]

In 1990 the Voters Organized to Expand Registration (VOTER) coalition consisting of citizen groups,[19] political and party activists,[20] and politicians[21] initiated a "two-pronged" offensive to "bring down the walls, and reduce the number of hoops one must jump through to register." The key was to get VOTER's proposed measures through the Arizona state assembly, building bipartisan coalitions in the Republican-dominated House and the Democrat-dominated Senate and finding a middle ground that would satisfy conservative Republicans. Using the formal legal approach, a legislative proposal (House Bill 2659), and a grassroots citizen initiative approach, VOTER proposed election-day registration and mail-in registration.[22]

The notion of changing Arizona's voter registration system to election-day registration was first discussed in 1970 and since has been a hot and controversial issue among Arizona's public officials. However, one of the benefits of having election-day registration is that it exempts states from the National Voter Registration Act.

Helen Hudgens, Coconino County recorder, was only one of two Arizona county officials to support the proposal of election-day registration back in 1970. Hudgens was concerned with the election procedures county recorders used to verify the eligibility of voters at the polls and the high expectations placed on volunteer poll workers to follow procedures pertaining to voter challenges. According to Hudgens, challenges seem to be aimed at people who appear on an inactive list. In actuality, any voter can be challenged. Challenges are very disruptive, and intimidating. I can think of no more chilling effect on voter turnout than the fact that voters may be challenged on election day. Not as a remote possibility, but an encouraged activity, it [challenges] has been used in the past very effectively to keep minority and low-income voters from going to the polls in Maricopa County.[23]

Hudgens felt that the misuse of election procedures concerning voter eligibility "can deny people the right to vote."[24]

Both political parties may have been advocating election-law reform, but they differed on the magnitude of reform they were seeking. On the issue of election-day registration, Kurt Davis, executive director of the State Republican Party in 1990, cautioned against election-day registration, claiming "it poses a real danger of fraud. How would you know that I'm not registered in five places?"[25] Supporters of election-day registration argued that "with computers it is possible for the state to allow a voter to register on election day itself and still prevent ghost-voting and other famous frauds of past years."[26]

Dana Larsen, director of Arizona Common Cause, suggested that "having such a long period between registration and voting locks people out of the process and only tends to feed cynicism and apathy."[27] State Representative Debbie McCune (D-Phoenix) supported VOTER's reform proposals by stating that

the interest in elections is heightened when the issues get hot and the campaign literature starts coming in, and when they [potential voters] begin to talk to their neighbors about it [the election]. Unfortunately, those things usually occur after the 50-day registration residency deadline has passed and the unregistered are barred from voting.[28]

According to Patricia Jo Angelini, VOTER chairwoman,

people do not think about registering nearly two months before an election ... people attempt to register when the media report on upcoming races and issues, and when candidates knock on doors or mail campaign literature. Unfortunately, by that time registration for that election has ended.

Political candidates in the 1990 Secretary of State's race were divided along party lines on election-day registration.[29] Republican candidate State Treasurer Ray Rottas felt that "people aren't interested in an election fifty days before they go to the polls," however he was not an advocate of election-day voter registration. He believed that election-day registration "may invite fraud by tempting voters to travel from precinct to precinct to register and vote the same day."[30] Democratic candidate Jim Shumway at first agreed with Rottas and opposed

election-day registration.[31] Shumway altered his position on election-day registration after changes were made to a proposed initiative whereby "voters would
be required to produce a picture-identification card that contains his or her address before being allowed to vote," a procedure that would deter fraudulent voting. Shumway's Democratic opponent Jim Mahoney endorsed election-day
registration because "[it] makes sense in a mobile state like Arizona, where thousands move in and out of the state and change addresses each year."[32]

When the voters elected Mahoney on November 7, 1990, with 58 percent of
the vote, Arizonans apparently had mandated their new Secretary of State to
move forward with political-campaign and voter-registration reform. It should
not have been too difficult with a Democratic majority in the State Senate.[33]

THE LEGISLATURE TAKES ACTION

As the Arizona Legislature retuned to work in January of 1990, election-reform
measures were among the bills introduced in the legislative session.[34] A bipartisan effort in 1990 involving Senate Judiciary Committee Chairman Leo Corbet
(R-Phoenix) along with Jones Osborn (D-Yuma) offered two bills that would
ease Arizona's restrictive voter registration laws. Senate Bill 1507 would reduce
the number of days individuals were required to reside in the state before registering to vote. The bill proposed that the residency requirement be reduced to
twenty-nine days.[35] Prior to this, Arizona state law required individuals to reside
in the state fifty days before voting.[36] Arizona was the only state to cut off voter
registration fifty days before a general election. The second bill, Senate Bill
1526, recommended that Arizona adopt a mail-in voter registration system.[37]

In a political maneuver to ease restrictions on campaign contributions, both
bills were tied to a conditional enactment clause that required passage of four
campaign-finance bills before Senate Bills 1507 and 1526 could be enacted.[38]

In April, Senator Corbet, sponsor of the voter-registration bills, threatened
to block the proposed legislation from the Senate floor because the political-
action committee Common Cause continued to lobby to block campaign-funding
legislation. In addition, Judiciary-committee Democrats David Bartlett and Jones
Osborn promised to sponsor amendments modifying Corbet's proposed campaign-finance legislation. Senator Corbet was angered. "[It's] because of the
PACS that I'm not running the bills. I may be stubborn and an old bastard, but
that's the way it is." Corbet felt he had "consented to numerous changes to suit
critics . . . and finally it just got to the point where people from Common Cause
and others just wanted it their way or no way, so it's going to be no way."[39]

By the end of the legislative session, the only voter-registration bill to make
it through the road of passage was Senate Bill 1507, reducing the closing date on
registration to twenty-nine days. Senate Bill 1526, allowing for mail-in registration, died.[40] VOTER announced plans to return in 1991 to lobby the state legislature for mail-in registration and same-day registration.[41]

In 1991, Senate Bill 1390 proposed a reduction in the residency requirement, from twenty-nine days to twenty days; absentee voting in any election; and
mail-in voting in some elections. If enacted, individuals eighteen years of age or
older, residing in the state at least twenty days, would be able to go to a polling
place, show proof of identification, register to vote, and cast his/her vote at the
same time.

Arizona's legislators were divided along party lines on the reforms. Senate
Democrats supported the reforms, maintaining that the changes would increase
voter participation in elections, while Republicans opposed them, arguing that
they would increase the cost of elections, attract uninformed voters, and invite
voter fraud.[42]

Senate Republicans Tom Patterson (Phoenix) and Jim Buster (Yuma), were
concerned that proposed reforms would invite uniformed voters to the polls. Patterson believed that "people don't stay away from the polls because of cumbersome registration requirements, but because they haven't taken the time to
become informed about the candidates and issues." He maintained that "the value of a vote to further the cause of a democratic government depends on the care
and thought that have gone into that vote."[43] Senator Buster believed that individuals do not register to vote because "they're lazy, or apathetic, or they're cyn-
ical about the system." Senator Armando Ruiz (D-Phoenix) disagreed with the
Republican argument and stated that the uninformed voter argument "takes us
back to the day of the old literacy test," when voters were required to take a test
to determine if the individual was competent to cast his or her vote.[44] The administering of the literacy test was arbitrary and, as a prerequisite to voting, was
implemented to discourage minorities from exercising their right to vote.

Another concern of the Republican Party in reforming Arizona's election
laws was the issue of voter fraud.[45] Republican senator Tom Patterson (Phoenix)
believed that "delayed registration" prevents voter fraud, whereas Senator Chuck
Blanchard (D-Phoenix) disagreed and maintained that Bill 1390 is "a chance to
reduce opportunities for election fraud. . . . Instances of fraud are rare in most
states with election-day registration."[46] The Senate, in a 14 to 13 party-split vote,
passed Senate Bill 1390.

The House version of Senate Bill 1390 differed in that it allowed voter-
registration forms to be distributed at all city, county, state, and federal government buildings. In addition, the forms would be placed in telephone books, in-
serted in public service utility bills, and attached to placemats at fast-food
restaurants. The House version did not propose election-day registration but
would create an ad hoc committee to study whether voters should be allowed to
register and vote on election day. Also, the House version proposed an alternative purging procedure and permitted mail-in voting in local and school-district
elections.[47]

On June 8, 1991, Senate Bill 1390 was sent to the House-Senate Conference
Committee to be reconciled. Twelve days later a revised voter-registration bill
resurfaced.[48] Opposed by conservative Republicans, the Democrat-dominated

Senate passed revised Senate Bill 1390 by a 21 to 9 vote on June 21, 1991. The next day, the legislation passed the Republican-dominated House unopposed, 53 to 0.[49] On July 1, 1991, Governor Fife Symington signed Senate Bill 1390 into law, saying the changes should "vastly improve the process, making it easier for citizens to register and vote. It also will help clean up our voter-registration rolls without fear of disenfranchising voters."[50] Once enacted, Senate Bill 1390 allowed for the mailing of registration forms to individuals renewing their driver's license through the mail, thus eliminating the deputy-registrar system. The bill suspended the biennial purge with a registration-verification procedure that placed nonvoters on inactive status for up to four years. In addition, it created a committee to study legislation allowing election-day registration and allowed for mail-in ballots in special districts.[51]

MAIL-IN REGISTRATION

Registering to vote no longer required "voters to travel to the county elections office in downtown Phoenix or contact a local deputy registrar."[52] Under the mail-in registration process, a person completes a voter-registration form and mails the form to the nearest county recorder's office. If all the information on the form is correct, the person is eligible to vote in the upcoming election. Mail-in registration forms are located in most public offices, like libraries, post offices, colleges, etc.

Abandoning the deputy-registrar system for self-registration by mail would make it less cumbersome for individuals to register to vote and made the process less political. Arizona's deputy-registration system was considered an exclusive process that benefited the political parties, since deputy registrars were selected from a list of eligible and qualified voters in the precinct provided by each political party's county chairman, and appointment was based on the recommendation of the county chairman.[53] The deputy registrar system excluded voters who were not active party members, or individuals who were registered as Independents, from becoming deputy registrars.

According to one administrative respondent, "it was to the parties' advantage to have a lot of them [deputy registrars] because you had to send them out, or the person had to come in, in order to register; so the Democrats would have theirs and the Republicans would have theirs and you had these huge [voter registration] drives" that benefited both the Democrat and Republican parties.[54] However, "not everybody feels comfortable going to a political party, or driving to the county recorder's office, or having a stranger come to your home," according to Representative Susan Gerard (R-Phoenix).[55]

Public and party officials were at odds over eliminating the deputy-registrar system. Arizona's Secretary of State from 1988 to 1990, Republican Jim Shumway, felt that the deputy-registrar system was "adequate, if you knew what to do."[56] Maricopa County Republican Party Chairwoman Donna Flanigan believed that the party "makes it pretty convenient for people to register."[57] Maricopa

County Democratic Party Chairwoman Jeannie Cox disagreed. "Lawmakers should abolish Arizona laws that require deputy registrars to be appointed by political parties," she suggested. "Anyone should be allowed to take a county-administered test to become a registrar. Arizona should discard antiquated laws that prohibit state, county, and city employees from signing up voters."[58]

Theoretically, a deputy-registration system that provides the opportunity for any individual to become a deputy registrar, and one that does not limit the number of deputy registrars, should increase the number of registrants by two million voters.[59] Then again, Arizona's deputy-registrar system was a restrictive process that allowed only members of the political parties to become eligible to register individuals to vote in national and state elections.

MOTOR-VOTER PROGRAM

Voter-registration reforms began in the early 1980s with a motor-voter program and continued into the 1990s with more liberalized state-initiated reforms. Arizona had already implemented many of the federally mandated NVRA programs and only had to tweak their voter-registration programs to comply with NVRA.

In the 1980s, under Secretary of State Rose Moffort, efforts were made to develop a more uniform application of election laws. Arizona's county- and city-level election administrators formed a legislative steering committee for the purpose of "identifying problems with the election procedures and methods used in antiquated election laws," and "to put together a compilation of things to help make the election law a little better understood."[60] Coconino County recorder Helen Hudges and Yavapai County recorder Patsy Denny lobbied for voter-registration reforms such as mail-in registration and redefining absentee balloting as early balloting.[61] Reform was also boosted by "the advent of computer applications allowing us to go into a statewide voter list so that we could try to prevent multiple registrations and voter fraud."[62]

Arizona had a motor-voter program in place prior to the NVRA mandate. After NVRA, Arizona's motor-voter program evolved from a passive to a more active process. The effort to offer motor-voter registration began when State Representative John Kromko (D-Tucson) attempted but failed to gather the number of signatures needed to have a legislature-initiated motor-voter referendum placed on the 1980 election ballot. Kromko felt that his proposed initiative, which called for automatic registration of individuals possessing an Arizona's driver's license, may have "seemed too radical at the time."[63] After a string of failed attempts to get voter-registration legislation through the state legislature,[64] a citizen initiative resurfaced in 1982. Concerned with the expense placed on both political parties to reregister voters every two years, Les Miller, a Phoenix attorney, led the motor-voter initiative drive.[65] Once on the ballot, Arizonans approved the initiative by 347,559 votes (51 percent of the vote), and by March 1983 the Motor Vehicle Division (MVD) implemented motor-voter.[66]

An impediment to the implementation of motor-voter in Arizona was that under Arizona Statutes only the county recorder, a justice of the peace, or a deputy registrar could register individuals to vote.[67]

> Under a deputization state, in order to execute something like motor-voter you would actually have to have staff assistance in the completion of the voter registration application. So you would not be able to implement a state motor voter program in a deputization state without having all of the front line workers deputized, and then you would not be able to implement it without all of the front-line workers then actively asking and offering assistance to people, because people can not fill out the voter registration form themselves in a deputization state.[68]

Therefore, MVD driver's license employees had to be deputized as special deputy registrars to register drivers to vote in federal and state elections.[69]

Arizona's MVD offices offered a "two-step" process. If motor-vehicle patrons wanted to register to vote, they would indicate so by checking a box on their driver's license application. They were then required to complete two separate applications, the driver's license application and the voter-registration application. Both applications required the same personal information and required a special deputy registrar to register MVD patrons.[70]

Arizona's legislation regarding motor-voter registration was somewhat vague; it did not specifically require the driver's license examiner to ask each patron if they were registered to vote in Arizona.[71] Because the task was not integrated into the person's daily routine it could be easily overlooked. If personnel did remember to ask if the individual was registered to vote they did so haphazardly, thereby missing potential registrants.

Additional problems surfaced in the day-to-day operation of Arizona's newly implemented motor-voter program. According to testimony provided by Coconino County recorder Helen Hudgens to the U.S. House of Representatives Subcommittee on Elections, "Even though the driver's license examiners are all trained to be deputy registrars, they do not give accurate information to the voter." For example, some individuals registered as Independents only to find out later that they could not vote in the primaries. "Information about the primary was not given because the examiner was so busy with other duties and forms or because the examiner feared falling into a political discussion."

Another problem area was the return of completed registration forms. "It is not unusual for people to say they thought they were registered or their address was corrected automatically because that is what they were told at MVD."[72] One such applicant "believed that the state didn't want her to vote." While waiting to take her driver's license examination, the applicant filled out a voter-registration form to be eligible to vote in the upcoming 1988 presidential election. When election day came, the applicant went to the polls to vote only to be informed that she could not vote. The voter-registration application completed at the MVD office had not been returned to the county clerk's office. The applicant didn't get to vote.[73] In order to correct some of the problems associated with motor-voter registration, driver's license examiners would be expected to be "knowledgeable on voter laws and responsible for the return of registration forms," which is an unrealistic expectation.[74]

Once Arizona adopted mail-in registration in 1992, registering MVD patrons was taken out of the hands of the staff altogether. According to one executive respondent,

> when someone came in for a driver's license, what would happen is the worker would tell the applicant, "Oh, if you want to register to vote, there is a pile of mail-in forms sitting over there.[75]

Motor-voter registration was the first reform effort that targeted Arizona's antiquated election laws. Seven years later, Arizona's legislators initiated legislation that moved up the closing date to twenty-nine days, trimmed residency requirements to twenty-nine days, abandoned the deputy-registrar system for mail-in registration, redefined absentee voting to "early voting," and suspended the purging process.

SUSPENDING PURGING FOR NOT VOTING

Before the NVRA went into effect, Arizona was one of four states to purge voters after a general election.[76] The other three states were Nevada, New Mexico, and Wyoming. Arizona's laws regarding the cancellation of voters from the registration rolls have varied. In 1950 and 1960 if an elector did not vote in each even-year primary or general election, he/she was purged from the registration rolls.[77] In 1970 if an elector did not vote in the presidential general election or return a restoration card, he/she was removed from the registration rolls.[78] In 1972 if an elector did not vote in the general election or return the restoration card, he or she was purged.[79] Once the motor-voter initiative was enacted in 1983, if an elector did not vote in the general election or retain a valid Arizona driver's license, he or she was purged from the registration rolls.[80]

Maricopa County Recorder Helen Purcell stated that under Arizona law,

> If you have not voted in a general election, you are taken off the rolls. If you maintain a valid Arizona driver's license, you are immediately put back on [after a purge], so in essence we take off all those people who did not vote and who do not hold a valid Arizona driver's license.[81]

Arizona's law established a double standard. If you are old or poor or don't own a vehicle, then you can be purged from the voter-registration roster.

According to the U.S. Census, almost half of the U.S. residents moved within the previous five years.[82] Of those residents, one in five people moved outside the county they formerly resided in and are the people most likely to become deadwood.[83] Election officials in Arizona estimate that as many as 22 percent to 25 percent of voter registrations are considered deadwood or "phantom" voters.[84] Deadwood or phantom voters are voters who have moved within or out of Arizona but did not change their address; or registered voters who have died but remain on the registration rolls.[85] For election administrators, deadwood voters create file-maintenance and data-reporting problems. First, deadwood voters inflate voter totals; thus, voter-turnout levels appear misleadingly low. The estimated disparity between the current population surveys and state reports on the number of people who registered to vote and voted is between 4 percent and 12 percent for previous election years.[86] Second, deadwood voters increase the cost associated with storing and maintaining registration lists. Third, deadwood voters increase the cost of printing, postage, and payroll. State and counties are required to mail sample ballots and election material to all registered voters.[87] It is estimated that $1 million is spent each election year on so-called phantom voters.[88]

Theoretically, the state has a legal/official interest in maintaining a list of eligible voters. Maintaining the accuracy of voter registration by purging individuals who have moved out of the state or individuals that have died eliminates the potential for fraudulent voting.[89] On the other hand, the practice of purging individuals who do not vote regularly or who do not retain a valid Arizona driver's license prevents an estimated two million voters from casting their vote on election day.

According to the Department of Justice, "Minority registrants were more likely than other registrants to be purged." As a result, in 1987 the Justice Department stepped in and disallowed the state of Arizona from purging voters from the registration rolls.[90]

COMPLYING WITH THE NVRA

In preparation for the federally mandated NVRA, Arizona's legislature and election administrators "were actively working towards [election law] reforms."[91] According to one election director,

> They [the Justice Department] came to us [the Secretary of State] and said there are going to be a few aspects if you want to be exempt from [NVRA].... One is allowing people to register at motor-vehicle offices while they're getting their driver's license. We've done that. Second was to provide self-registration. Let everybody be his or her own deputy registrar, and do mail-in registration. Have agency-based registration, where we had it available at all the social services agencies. And four, to have a program where we had the ability to have voter-registration drives. We complied with all of those . . . so our big change will be that we will have public assistance agencies offering voter registration.[92]

In spite of taking the lead and reforming voter-registration procedures, Arizona was mandated to revise voter-registration methods to comply with the NVRA. Another election administrator stated,

> It was a very large surprise to me that Arizona, because we had been such good citizens at it . . . we had raised our ability to put registration out there, to all of the different segments of the community. We were then pushed into doing NVRA on a mandatory basis, with all their little rules and regulations, and we had complied with what they needed, because the only out was same-day [registration]. . . . It was a real shock, because we had played by all the rules.[93]

Since the aim of the NVRA was to encourage different publics, specifically disenfranchised publics, to register to vote, the Arizona Secretary of State's office, under Dick Mahoney, solicited administrators, directors, and managers from various public agencies and political and community organizations to work together on developing a strategic plan to meet the objectives of the NVRA.[94]

Before the NVRA, the MVD was offering a method-voter registration, "so it was not much of a change for them." From the beginning, public-assistance agencies were opposed to the NVRA, not just in Arizona but also nationally.[95] Their initial response was "there is no way we're going to do this [comply with the NVRA]."[96] The public-assistance agencies' main concern at first was their workload; they felt that they "have a high enough workload . . . [compliance with the NVRA] was one more thing that they would have to do," a natural response.[97] However, the time to debate whether or not agencies would offer voter registration was long gone. What needed to be addressed was "how are we going to do it [comply with the NVRA] so that it's beneficial for everyone."[98] What made a difference in getting the agencies to come onboard, according to one county recorder, "depended on how the recorders in their respective counties . . . worked with them [agencies], in regards to what was working and what was not working, and what problems are you [agencies] having, so it can be avoided."[99] During the planning of the NVRA, public officials expressed some concern regarding the potential impact mail-in registration might have on language minorities, and the effect of public assistance agency registration on undocumented workers.

In order to comply with the NVRA language requirement, the task force committee recommended: 1, bi-lingual posters be placed in areas to advise people that voter registration services are available[100]; 2, bilingual audio cassettes and translators should be available to provide language minorities with voter-registration information[101]; and 3, the Secretary of State's office will have a bilingual toll-free telephone number providing oral instructions on voter-registration procedures.[102]

The Secretary of State's office, in cooperation with Arizona's counties, provides language minorities with assistance on voter registration. The committee felt that agencies and organizations not mandated by the NVRA but designated by county recorders to distribute and collect mail-in voter registration forms should not "be burdened with the mandates of providing language assistance."[103] They recommended that minority-language questions should be directed to each county recorder's office and should not be responded to by public-assistance staff.[104]

Another area of concern expressed at the public forum was the impact the NVRA might have on undocumented workers from Mexico, Canada, or other countries. One public assistance program manager stated, "Undocumented workers might be fearful of applying if they thought that answering questions on the application might jeopardize their position."[105] Citizenship is not required to participate in some public-assistance programs, but it is required to register to vote. According to a public assistance program manager, "The minute you start to ask if you are a U.S. citizen or any implication thereof, it is going to cause word to be put out in the street that the Federales are here. . . . This type of error [will cause] a drop in [public-assistance program] participation quickly."[106] The manager also stated, "Since this [the NVRA] is a mandatory law, and the public-assistance programs don't have a choice whether we want to participate or not, every consideration needs to be taken to know the program and also the participants when the laws governing implementation are formed."[107] The public-assistance manager expressed concern with the language barrier of those applying for benefits and suggested that there is a need for more bilingual personnel.[108]

The language barrier continues to affect Latino and Native American populations. Providing bilingual election material and assistance at all phases of the electoral process diminishes the language barrier that often impedes their political progress and limits Latino and Native American voter participation. Since Arizona adopted mail-in registration and early voting, reduced residency and closing-date requirements, abandoned the deputy-registrar system, and suspended the purging process in 1992, and adopted an active motor-voter program in 1996, voter turnout should have increase among previously disenfranchised populations, especially the Latino population.

NOTES

1. Executive Director, *Telephone Interview*, March 10, 1997.
2. Steve Yozwiak, "Governor Runoff Set for Feb. 26, U.S. Approval of Election Law Is Expected," *The Arizona Republic,* 20 November 1990: A1.
3. Charles L. Cotrell, "Assessing the Effects of the U.S. Voting Rights Act," *Publius* 16, No. 4 (1986), pp. 5–16.
4. Ibid. [The same page as the preceding note]
5. Flannery, "Election Reforms Bill Signed," B1.
6. Ibid. [The same page as the preceding note]
7. "Navajos Lack Voting Rights, U.S. Suit Says," *The Arizona Republic*, 9   December 1988, A1.
8. Ibid. [The same page as the preceding note]
9. "Loud and Strong Recall Credited as County Voter List Swells," *The Phoenix Gazette*, 20 April 1988, A1.
10. "Navajos Lack Voting Rights, U.S. Suit Says," *The Arizona Republic*, 9   December 1988, A1.
11. Steve Yozwiak and Ed Foster, "Reply to 'AzScam' Legislation Ok'd Lobbyist Reins as Key Reform," *The Arizona Republic*, 10 November 1991, A1.
12. "Party Activists, Former Officials to Study Problems in County Elections Operation," *The Phoenix Gazette,* 15 December 1988, B9.
13. "Loud and Strong Recall Credited as County Voter List Swells," *The Phoenix Gazette*, 20 April, 1988, A1.
14. Steve Yozwiak, "Registering: Bump on Road to Polls 'Motor Voter' Helps Expand Rolls Election," *The Arizona Republic*, 16 July 1990, A1.
15. Elections director, personal interview by Elaine Rodriquez, 18 June 1996; and a county recorder, personal interview by Elaine Rodriquez, 17 June 1996.
16. The committee was headed by Maricopa County Recorder Helen Purcell, which included political party activists Doug Collier and Mike Bomar representing the Republican Party, Marcia Imber representing the Democratic Party, and Ken Van Doren representing the Libertarian Party, along with former Elections Director Jim Riggs and former City Clerk Donna Culbertson. See "Party Activists, Former Officials to Study Problems in County Elections Operation," *The Phoenix Gazette,* 15 December 1988, B9.
17. "Navajos Lack Voting Rights, U.S. Suit Says," *The Arizona Republic*, 9   December 1988, A1.
18. "Ed Buck Seeks Open Primaries, Election-Day Voter Registration," *The Arizona Republic,* 24 April 1989, B1; and "Loud and Strong Recall Credited as County Voter List Swells," *The Phoenix Gazette,* 20 April 1988, A1.
19. The citizen-interest groups included Common Cause (a political-watchdog group), AFL-CIO, and the Southwest Voter Registration Project. See "Wide-Open Voter Registration Pushed by Activist Coalition," *Arizona Capitol Times*, 21 February 1990, vol. 91, issue 5, pg. 2.

20. Political activist Louis Hoffman, an attorney at Brown & Bain Law Firm in Phoenix; and party activist Patricia Jo Patricia, a public-health lobbyist, former state Democratic party official, and chairwoman of VOTE. Ibid, p. 2.

21. Politicians include Pima County Supervisor Greg Lunn, State Representatives John Kromko and Armando Ruiz (sponsor of HB2659), and former Governor Bruce Babbitt. See Ibid. [The same page as the preceding note]

22. "Wide-Open Voter Registration Pushed by Activist Coalition," p. 2; and Steve Yozwiak, "Two-Pronged Campaign is Launched to Allow Voter Registration," *The Arizona Republic,* 20 February 1990, C10.

23. U.S. Congress, House, *Voter Registration: Testimony from Helen I. Hudgens, Recorder*, Coconino County, Arizona, pp. 762–790.

24. Ibid. p. 770.

25. "Wide-Open Voter Registration Pushed by Activist Coalition," 2; and "Two-Pronged Campaign Is Launched to Allow Voter Registration," C10.

26. Ibid. p. 2.

27. Steve Yozwiak, "Two-Pronged Campaign Is Launched to Allow Voter Registration," C10.

28. Ibid. p. C10.

29. "Election-day voter registration" and "same-day voter registration" are used interchangeably.

30. Carol Sowers and Jim Walsh, "A Lesson in Getting Out Vote Minnesota Cuts Red Tape Election '90," *The Arizona Republic,* 17 July 1990, A1.

31. Pat Flannery, "Same-day Registration Gets Shumway Support," *The Phoenix Gazette,* 7 April 1990, B1.

32. Sowers and Walsh, "A Lesson in Getting Out Vote Minnesota Cuts Red Tape Election '90," A1.

33. Maren Bingham, "Mahoney Eager to Start, New Secretary of State Sees Many Changes," *The Phoenix Gazette,* 7 November 1990, A4; and Mike Padgett, "Shumway Has No Time to Ease into New Post, Plans Several Changes in Elections Job," *The Phoenix Gazette*, 3 December 1990, B1.

34. "Election 'Reform' Hot Topic; Registration Date Leads List," *Arizona Capitol Times,* 3 January 1990, section, front.

35. Steve Yozwiak, "Measure to Ease Limits on Campaign Gift Gains," *The Arizona Republic*, 10 March 1990, B1.

36. Arizona, *Revised Statutes, Annotated* (1992), p. 5.

37. Steve Yozwiak, "Measure to Ease Limits on Campaign Gift Gains," B1.

38. "Election-Reform Package Bogs Down in Senate," *Arizona Capital Times*, 11 April 1990, pp. 1–2.

39. Ibid. p. 2.

40. "Don't Let These Bills Die," *The Phoenix Gazette*, 9 June 1990, A12; and "Voter Registration Process can be Made Easier Yet," *The Arizona Republic*, 1 July 1990, C4.

41. Sowers and Walsh, "A Lesson in Getting Out Vote Minnesota Cuts Red Tape Election '90," A1.

42. Sean Griffin, "Voter Sign-up Bill Gets Tentative OK, Measure Relaxes Restrictions," *The Phoenix Gazette*, 5 April 1991, A6.

43. Ibid., p. A6.

44. "Constituent Communications Limit Advances in Election-Reform Fight." *Arizona Capitol Times*, 10 April 1991, pp. 3–4.

45. Fraud associated with voter-registration laws is voting using a false identity and address. The occasional voter who casts his or her vote in the wrong polling place is not viewed as committing fraudulent behavior, since the action is associated with carelessness or being misinformed rather than a deliberate act.

46. Griffin, "Voter Sign-up Bill Gets Tentative OK, Measure Relaxes Restrictions," A6.

47. Steve Yozwiak, "Mail-In Registration for Voters Is Backed," 16 May 1991, B13.

48. Mike Padgett, "Mail-In Voter Registration Mulled Bill Would Ease Sign-Up, Save Money, Correct Inaccurate Rolls," *The Phoenix Gazette*, 8 June 1991, A8.

49. "House Approves Bill on Registering to Vote by Mail," *The Arizona Republic*, 22 June 1991, A10.

50. Pat Flannery, "Election Reforms Bill Signed," *The Phoenix Gazette*, 2 July 1991, B1.

51. Ibid., B1.

52. Election director, personal interview, June 18, 1996.

53. Arizona, *Revised Statutes, Annotated* (1992), p. 1.

54. Election director, personal interview, June 18, 1996.

55. Steve Yozwiak, "Registering: Bump on Road to the Polls, 'Motor Voter' Helps Expand Rolls Election 90," A1.

56. Ibid. [The same page as the preceding note]

57. Ibid. [The same page as the preceding note]

58. Sowers and Walsh, "A Lesson in Getting Out Vote Minnesota Cuts Red Tape Election '90," A1.

59. *Committee for the Study of the American Electorate*, pp. 583–601.

60. Male elections director, personal interview by Fred Solop, 29 July 1994.

61. Female elections director, personal interview by Fred Solop, 29 July 1994.

62. Male elections director, personal interview by Fred Solop, 29 July 1994.

63. Steve Yozwiak, "Registering: Bump on Road to the Polls, 'Motor Voter' Helps Expand Rolls Election 90," *The Arizona Republic*, 16 July 1990: A1.

64. Frances Fox Piven and Richard A. Cloward, *Why Americans Don't Vote*, (New York: Pantheon Books, 1988), p. 221.

65. Steve Yozwiak, "Registering: Bump on Road to the Polls, 'Motor Voter' Helps Expand Rolls Election 90," A1.

66. Fred Solop and Susan Nicholls, *Motor Voter: Toward Universal Registration* (New York: Human SERVE, 1986), p. 9.

67. A deputy registrar is an eligible voter duly qualified and appointed by the county recorder to register individuals to vote in state and federal elections. See Arizona, *Revised Statutes, Annotated* (1992), p. 27.

68. Executive director, telephone interview by Elaine Rodriquez, 10 March 1997.

69. A special deputy registrar is a driver's license examiner duly qualified and appointed by the county recorder to register individuals to vote in state and federal elections. See Arizona, *Revised Statutes, Annotated* (1992), p. 14.

70. Yozwiak, "Registering: Bump on Road to the Polls, 'Motor Voter' Helps Expand Rolls Election 90," A1.

71. Solop and Nicholls, *Motor Voter: Toward Universal Registration*, p. 8.

72. U. S. Congress, House, *Voter Registration: Testimony from Helen I. Hudgens, Recorder, Coconino County, Arizona*, Subcommittee on Elections of the Committee on House Administration. 100th Congress, 2nd Session (Washington, D.C.: U.S. Government Printing Office, 1989), pp. 762–790.

73. "State's Miles of Red Tape Driving License Applicant to Despair," *The Arizona Republic*, 24 February 1989: B1.

74. U.S. Congress, House, *Voter Registration: Testimony from Helen I. Hudgens, Recorder*, Coconino County, Arizona, pp. 762–790.

75. Executive director, telephone interview by Elaine Rodriquez, 10 March 1997.

76. Election director, personal interview, June 18, 1996.

77. Ibid. [The same page as the preceding note]

78. Ibid. [The same page as the preceding note]

79. Ibid. [The same page as the preceding note]

80. Mike Padgett, "Invalid Voter Registrations Cost State," *The Phoenix Gazette*, 14 September 1990; and "Reform Urged to Rid Voter Roll Deadwood," *The Arizona Republic*, 18 September 1988, B1.

81. Mike Padgett, "Mail-In Voter Registration Mulled Bill Would Ease Sign-Up, Save Money, Correct Inaccurate Rolls," *The Phoenix Gazette*, 8 June 1991, A8.

82. "Geographical Mobility: 1995 to 2000," *Census 2000 Brief*, 2003.

83. Michael P. McDonald, "Is Voter Registration Up Everywhere in America?" *Report by the Brookings Institute*, 2004.

84. Mike Padgett, "Invalid Voter Registrations Cost State," A1; and Padgett, "Mail-In Voter Registration Mulled Bill Would Ease Sign-Up, Save Money, Correct Inaccurate Rolls," A8.

85. "Reform Urged to Rid Voter Roll Deadwood," *The Arizona Republic*, 18 September 1988, B1.

86. U.S. Bureau of the Census, "Voting and Registration in the Election of November 2004," *Current Population Reports*, 2006, p. 14.

87. Mike Padgett, "Mail-In Voter Registration Mulled Bill Would Ease Sign-Up, Save Money, Correct Inaccurate Rolls," A8.

88. Mike Padgett, "Invalid Voter Registrations Cost State," A1.

89. Ibid. [The same page as the preceding note]

90. Steve Yozwiak, "Registering: Bump on Road to the Polls, 'Motor Voter' Helps Expand Rolls Election 90," A1; and Padgett, "Invalid Voter Registrations Cost State," A1.

91. Election director, personal interview, July 29, 1994.

92. Election director, personal interview, June 18, 1996.

93. Ibid. [The same page as the preceding note]

94. The task force included intergovernmental agencies responsible for administering the NVRA, such as the Secretary of State, county recorders, MVD, and public-assistance agencies. Also, community-based organizations that directly offered services to disenfranchised publics, such as the Maricopa County NAACP, the Advocate for Independent Living, the Intertribal Council, and the Hispanic Chamber of Commerce were asked to participate. In addition, political organizations that take an active role in registering individuals to vote, such as the League of Women Voters, the League of Arizona Cities and Towns, and Maricopa County Democrat and Republican Party chairs, were included in the discussions, and, finally, individuals who would be responsible for initiating the legislation, such as state senators, representatives, and the Attorney General's office.

The task force was divided into three subcommittees: 1, the Public Assistance Agency Committee; 2, the Voter File Maintenance and the Fail-Safe Voting Committee; and 3, the MVD and County Data Processing Committee. Committees were asked to design implementation plans for each of the designated NVRA voter registration agencies. In addition to committee meetings, two public hearings were held, one in Tucson and the other in Phoenix, to solicit public opinion regarding the implementation of the NVRA.[94] The task force served as an apparatus to establish "standardized procedures." The different agencies affected by the law were asked to provide input regarding their particular needs. According to an elections director, "Everyone was much more willing to do it [comply with the NVRA] . . . it was not forced down upon them."

95. Ibid. [The same page as the preceding note]

96. Ibid. [The same page as the preceding note]

97. County Recorder, personal interview, June 17, 1996.

98. Ibid. [The same page as the preceding note]

99. Ibid. [The same page as the preceding note]

100. *Task Force Meeting: National Voter Registration Act*, 1 December 1993.

101. *Task Force Meeting: Public Assistance Agency Group*, 17 November 1993.

102. *Task Force Meeting: National Voter Registration Act*, 1 December 1993.

103. *Task Force Meeting: Summary of Subcommittees Reports*, 14 December 1993.

104. *Task Force Meeting: National Voter Registration Act Interim Committee*, 14 June 1994.

105. *Public Hearing*, The National Voter Registration Act, conducted by Margaret Steers, Donna Nolan, Jim Shumway, 13 December 1993, Central Library Auditorium, Phoenix, Arizona; and Public Assistance Program Manager, Personal Interview by Elaine Rodriquez, July 25, 1996.

106. Public Assistance Program Manager, personal interview by Elaine Rodriquez, July 25, 1996.

107. Ibid. [The same page as the preceding note]

108. Ibid. [The same page as the preceding note]

CHAPTER FOUR

THE IMPACT OF THE NVRA

> The National Voter Registration Act only works when people who implement
> the programs are willing to make it work.
>
> —A county recorder—

The National Voter Registration Act has met with some resistance and much criticism. Several state and county officials viewed the NVRA as a federal intrusion on states' rights,[1] while public-assistance managers viewed NVRA as creating more paperwork.[2] The following scenarios presented to an election administrator express the perspective of public assistance case managers:

> Scenario 1: Our offices [referring to public-assistance agencies] have so many people coming in for services that routinely about once a day the fire marshall comes in and makes us remove people from the building. We have glass all the way around the people and they talk through these little holes. I haven't had an employee that's not been shot, stabbed, or attacked. You can be assured that I will just say, "Could you excuse me, would you like to register to vote?"[3]

> Scenario 2: A caseworker who was responsible for taking the children from abusive situations and putting them in foster homes said, as I'm wrenching that child out of the mothers arms, I will say, "Excuse me, could I get you to register to vote?" It is ludicrous.[4]

NVRA was enacted to "level the playing field"[5] by enfranchising citizens who previously had been estranged from the electoral process. To achieve this end, states were mandated to offer voter registration at all governmental agencies. Theoretically, NVRA should have increased voter registration and turnout. However, the actual practice, or how state agencies implement and administer NVRA, determine its effectiveness as an election-reform strategy.

NVRA: State and County Agency Perspectives

County Recorders' Perspectives

County recorders in Arizona were asked how successful NVRA has been in achieving its objective to increase the number of eligible citizens who register to vote in elections. More than two-thirds (67 percent) of the county recorders responding to the survey[6] felt that NVRA was somewhat to very successful in achieving its objectives, while one-third of the county recorders felt that NVRA was not successful at all at achieving its objectives. Respondents felt that the impact of NVRA would be more positive at the national level than in Arizona, since Arizona already had many of the NVRA requirements in place. Three county recorders noted no significant increase in voter registration in their counties.

County recorders were asked to express their level of satisfaction with NVRA. A majority (55 percent) of the county recorders were somewhat to very dissatisfied with NVRA. They felt that 1, NVRA caused more confusion for the voter; 2, the agencies were not cooperative; 3, the additional amount of record keeping and tracking required was excessive; 4, it resulted in additional paperwork for the agencies; and 5, Arizona had similar programs already in place. For the most part county recorders and election-director respondents expressed dissatisfaction with NVRA record-keeping requirements, the tracking of registrants, and the declination process.[7] Two-fifths (44 percent) of the county recorders were somewhat to very satisfied with NVRA.

Section 9 of the NVRA requires the Federal Election Commission to submit a written report to Congress assessing "the impact of this act on the administration of elections for Federal office . . . including recommendations for improvements in federal and state procedures, forms, and matters affected by this act."[8] In order to comply with Section 9 of the NVRA, state election officials require county recorders to track the number of voter-registration applications from each participating agency. County recorders must keep records on the number of new registrants, the number of registrants changing their registration information, the number of duplicate registration applications, the number of registrants who were deleted from the registration lists, and the number of confirmation mailings and responses received.[9]

The main problem county recorders mentioned regarding NVRA recordkeeping provisions had to do with data processing. Not all of Arizona's county recorder's offices have a computerized system for maintaining voter-registration information. Therefore they must compile the requested reporting information manually, requiring additional employees or adding to the workload of existing employees. The counties that have a computerized system had to create database programs for maintaining and reporting required voter registration information. This created an additional expense to the county and state because NVRA is an unfunded mandate.

Election directors and county recorders alike feel that the declination form scares applicants and adds paperwork for both the applicants and the agencies "without a markedly successful return on the effort."[10] According to one director, applicants were concerned that if they responded that they did not want to register to vote, they would not receive services. "It scares some of the people, especially if their language skills are not real good in English. We have to reassure them but they're still scared,"[11] Even though the declaration form specifically states, "Applying to register to vote or declining will not affect the amount of assistance that you will be provided by this agency,"[12] in both the English and Spanish.

In some of the agencies the numbers of declination forms were 3-to-1 with registration applications.[13] However, the number of declarations an agency reports is not a true reflection of actual clients served or services rendered. For instance, if one individual accessed different agencies and had already registered to vote, then that person probably filled-out several declination forms, depending on how may agencies that person visited.[14] Also, if an individual accessed one agency multiple times, or had already registered to vote, that individual must fill out a declination form every time thereafter, "even if the service provider knew that they registered the individual the last time they were requesting services.[15]

One public-assistance manager stated,

As far as having the registration forms available and handing them out, we have no problem with that. We are happy to do that and process them through our system. But this declination form just seems to be a waste of time and a waste of paper. It is the greatest irritation, and as far as we are concerned it has no usefulness in the process.[16]

The official purpose of the declaration form was to promote a "staff-active" voter registration process within the public assistance and MVD agencies, so that the same level of assistance would be provided toward the completion of the voter-registration form as it is provided toward the completion of all other applications.[17] According to an executive director of a national nonprofit nonpartisan voter registration organization, the declination form,

builds in an assurance that every person is being asked if they want to register to vote. We felt that the question must be in writing because otherwise if you leave the prompt question as a verbal prompt and not a written prompt, it would just depend on the memory of the staff person to remember to ask each person, "Do you want to register to vote?" Our goal has been to permanently integrate voter registration into the routine activities of that agency. The way to accomplish permanent integration is to have it in writing on the form.[18]

As the NVRA moved through Congress, Senate Republicans were concerned that agency-based applicants might feel coerced. Senator Duraburg (R-Minnesota) believed that welfare recipients were more vulnerable than other populations to feel as if they were being coerced to fill out the form in a certain way, so he wanted a warning reduced to writing.[19] So the "I accept or I decline" statement to satisfy election reformists, the "I have not been coerced" statement to satisfy Republicans, and "Your declination will not in any way affect your benefits" statement to satisfy public-assistance agencies all became part of a separate declination form.[20]

There was another problem associated with the tracking of declination forms according to two election directors. "We have to report the number of registration forms by category. How do you keep track of the source of the form without revealing the source of registration?"[21] According to one elections administrator,

> NVRA tracking is "unconscionable." The very fact that we have to track people is a personal threat to women, because women are the ones that are usually applying for these services [public assistance]. Now voter-registration files are tagged, so that I can report to the feds how many voter-registration forms are from AFDC—a stigma that never leaves the registrant's file, even if they make it out of the welfare system.[22]

State administrators are working to get the law changed. Said one county recorder, "The Secretary of State's office has mechanisms for keeping track of the number of people who register to vote and the number who do not register to vote. Keeping track of individuals who do not register to vote through the declaration process seems irrational."[23]

County recorders were also asked to assess (using a scale of 1 to 5, with 1 representing poor and 5 representing excellent) how cooperative and efficient other agencies—the Motor Vehicle Division (MVD), public-assistance agencies, and disability agencies—have been in processing and forwarding voter registration applications to county offices. Eighty-eight percent of the county recorders felt that the public assistance agencies were more effective at processing and forwarding voter-registration applications than the MVD (76 percent) and the disability agencies (63 percent), while three-quarters (76 percent) of the county recorders felt that public-assistance agencies were more efficient at processing and forwarding voter-registration applications than the MVD (63 percent) and the disability agencies (50 percent). This was a surprise, since the MVD has had motor-voter registration in effect since 1983. One would assume that they would be better at processing and forwarding voter-registration applications than public assistance agencies, however it appears that this is not the case.

County recorders were asked which of the NVRA reforms had the most influence on increasing voter registration in their county. One-third of the recorders felt that motor-voter and mail-in registration combined had the most influence, while 22 percent felt that motor-voter registration alone had the most influence and 11 percent felt that mail-in registration alone had the most influence on voter registration. One-third of the county recorders felt that the NVRA reforms had no influence whatsoever on voter-registration rates.

Finally, county recorders were asked to provide suggestions on how the law could be improved. Again, one county recorder suggested that the declination form requirement should be eliminated. Two county recorders mentioned the costs associated with voter registration, including the increase in voter registration forms for distribution and computer applications. Even though in 1996 the post office provides a special rate of 8 cents for mailing out voter-registration cards, "If it doesn't reach its destination, it can cost up to 80 cents to get it back."[24]

The main problems county recorders mentioned in regards to NVRA programs were 1, receiving incomplete forms, and 2, the failure to receive forms in a timely manner. These problems require county recorders to allocate more time to registrants than they would normally. When county recorders receive incomplete registration applications, follow-up with the registrant to complete the registration application becomes necessary.

PUBLIC ASSISTANCE AGENCY PERSPECTIVES

According to the county recorders and election directors I interviewed, there were some initial grumblings from the public-assistant agencies about NVRA requirements. They viewed them as "just one more thing for them to do."[25]

The public-assistance managers interviewed admitted that mandating their agencies to offer voter registration did not go over well initially. There was a lot of animosity. Two of the public-assistance administrators interviewed stated, "Every time the legislature meets we have more things put upon us by the feds and the state. We see it [NVRA] as the law, and we will comply with the law."[26] According to one manger,

> We are not salesmen, selling the voter-registration act. We make a legitimate effort to offer it [voter registration] to everyone. We provide a service to people in need. . . . A lot of them could really care less [about registering to vote]. They are looking at where their next hamburger is coming from, not who is going to be in Congress.[27]

Another public assistance program manager stated,

> One of the things that we do verify is residency, and the voter-registration card is one of the acceptable documents for both state and county residency. Traditionally, the department [public assistance] has done quite a bit of registration, back before the mail-in program came in. The majority of the staff were deputy registrars, we trained in mass, and it was particularly useful. We would be able to register them and facilitate that process for them, and that way we could then get a residency document.[28]

So for this department the method of offering voter-registration services was already in practice, which perhaps accounts for the small numbers of public-assistance registrants reported to the state.[29]

Public assistance agency enrollment varies according to the type of service. According to two program managers, their offices see about two thousand to three thousand individuals in a month.[30] "That doesn't represent the full number of applications we received because there are a variety of ways the applications can be started."[31] Another manager said that about six thousand applications are given out per month.[32]

According to the public assistance program managers, in 90 percent of the cases clients are offered the opportunity to register to vote both visually and verbally. First, when the applicant enters the office, the receptionist hands them a premade package of applications. Then the client is verbally asked if they wish to register to vote during the interview process. Clients are given the option of either filling out the voter-registration form in the office, with the assistance of the interviewer, or the client can take the form home to complete and mail it in.

Public-assistance agencies have had different experiences with their clientele. Some interviewers find that most people will choose to just take the form home with them, whereas others are finding that they're actually filling out most of the paperwork in the office.[33] One public-assistance supervisor stated, "The majority of the clients will fill it out here and have us mail the form in. Only about two percent take the form with them."[34]

The voter-registration process can take anywhere between 2 to 5 minutes for each client, which does not seem like a great amount of time, but the thousands of applications processed per month can add up to "a good hour out of a person's work day," especially "when they could have been doing [public-assistance] stuff, which is why we are here is the first place."[35] According to the public-assistance administrators interviewed, most of the people requesting social services are concerned not with registering to vote but with either health-care coverage for their child or food for their family.

Ultimately about two-thirds of the applicants decline to register to vote. The reason given most often is that they are already registered.[36] One public-assistance manager stated, "Perhaps twenty to thirty people a day would actually want a registration form. The average is about one a day per site that clients actually say, 'Yes, I want to register.' The majority of people tell us that they are already registered to vote."[37]

All of the managers interviewed felt that offering voter-registration services at their agencies would not have a significant impact on increasing voter participation. One manager did agree that "we may register some folks that might have slipped though the cracks, so we may increase the numbers a little bit. However, I don't think it is going to change people's attitudes once they're registered and increase participation in the election process."[38] Another manager stated that clients

> will have the opportunity once, twice, or three times a day to register to vote. They are probably getting bombarded with voter-registration forms. We get people who say, "Oh no, I've done that, why do you keep asking me if I want to register to vote?" They get irritated. People come to see us to get medical care. Registering to vote has got to be the second or third or fourth, way down the line in importance.[39]

Another manager stated,

> Their main goal is to get their public- assistance checks. They did not
> come in to vote or register to vote. If they have to agree to something to
> get those checks, they are going to do it, and take it home and throw it
> in the garbage. I am sure a small percentage might be interested in it.[40]

Most of the public-assistance managers interviewed felt that completing, ac-
cumulating, storing, and routing of forms was a waste of time and money. One
manager felt that offering voter registration at all public assistance agencies was
a duplication of services. He suggested, "They should have picked one main
agency, because the same people who are on food stamps are probably on [other
public-assistance programs] and vice versa."[41]

THE IMPACT OF NVRA ON LATINO COMMUNITIES

According to the NVRA, "Discriminatory and unfair registration laws and procedures can have a direct and damaging effect on voter participation in elections
for federal office and disproportionately harm voter participation by various
groups, including racial minorities."[42] NVRA programs were created to provide
additional voter-registration opportunities to previously disenfranchised racial
minorities, such as the Latino community. With this in mind, county recorders
and election directors were asked to comment on the impact of NVRA programs
on Latino communities.

Only three of the nine county recorders (33 percent) felt that voter registration numbers increased for the Latino population, compared to 22 percent of the
recorders, who felt that Latino voter registration remained the same. One county
recorder was unsure of the impact of the NVRA on Hispanic voter registration
numbers, and three recorders did not respond to the question. One county recorder commented that increased Latino voter registration was due in part to
increases in the Latino population and not the NVRA. Other recorders commented that traditional methods of voter registration, such as voter-registration
drives or Latino special interest groups, probably have more influence than reformed voter registration programs such as NVRA.

County recorders and election directors expressed concern about Latinos'
poor participation levels. Some recorders felt the reasons for poor participation
levels among Latinos were 1, they lack an understanding of the political process;
2, a large segment of the Latino community is noncitizen; and 3, they have a
misconception that "if they register to vote and then do vote they will get called
for jury duty."[43] According to one county recorder, Latinos don't make the connection between the decision politicians make and the direction of their community. The decisions politicians make do affect the Latino community, such as the
jobs that will be provided, the roads that will be built, and the parks that will be
provided for their children.[44]

Another county recorder stated, "We provide the same services to the Latino community that we provide to any other community." For example, in the Hispanic areas of the counties, voter registration and election information is provided in Spanish and is announced on the Spanish radio and television stations. One country recorder mentioned, "We had an early voting site in the heart of the area [Latino sector] and it was the worst turnout as far as people participating." Another county recorder stated that when she ran for elected office, she mainly concentrated on middle-to-upper class registered voters, the possible switches. She did not concentrate on the Hispanic voter because "it's too hard to get them to vote."

Some of the situations Latinos encounter possibly discourage them from fully participating in the electoral process. One of the biggest problems reported by a county recorder involved the usage of names. In the Spanish culture, women honor their heritage by using the maiden surnames of both parents and then their married surname. For example, my legal name would be Maria Rodriguez-Baca-Lucero. When it comes to registering to vote, Latinas register under their legal name. At the election precinct, often the election personnel have to look under three different names before they locate the ballot. It delays the process and it seems "like they registered twice." So for the ease of voting, Latinas are asked to select, for "American purposes," a first name and last name. According to the recorder, "I want to make sure that they understand that we are not trying to disinherit any family member, but at least for voting purposes they need to select one surname so they won't be embarrassed in the polling place by someone trying to challenge their vote."[45] For the Latina registrant it's an uncomfortable situation to face for the purpose of voting. It challenges her cultural belief and privacy and may discourage her from participating in the electoral process.

Comments presented by the county recorders clearly suggest that NVRA, as an election-reform strategy designed to increase voter-registration rates among Latinos, is somewhat suspect and probably not as effective as hoped. In order to topple the tribulations confronting the Latino nonvoting community, additional support and outreach programs, such as a voter-educational component specifically targeted at the Latino community, is essential.

How fervent voter registration was portrayed was a concern expressed by one public-assistance manger. If registering to vote is strongly promoted by the public-assistance agencies, noncitizens and undocumented applicants seeking emergency services might be too intimidated to apply for services, especially if the image projected implies the involvement of a governmental authority or "police action,"[46] a perception that deters some individuals from seeking pubic-assistance services.

However, not all public-assistance managers shared that concern. Others felt that through word of mouth, individuals in their community know what services they need to apply for and the documentation needed to apply for those services.[47] "Occasionally, a client will ask, 'Do I have to register to vote to receive services?' and we have to reassure them that declining to register to vote does not affect the services they can receive."[48] According to one manager,

We have measurements of the number of applications taken six months before this [NVRA] went into effect and six months after. There is no change in the number, so there certainly is no substantial problem in terms of them being forced away or feeling that they have to do something, because there was no change in the effect of the applications as far as we can tell. There seems to be no change. If we had a drop of 10 percent then we would have to wonder if it is because we are doing something different. There is no change, so there is no reason for us to suspect any problem.[49]

County recorders and election directors believed that NVRA works only when people who implement the programs are willing to make it work. Many considered NVRA to be a federal intrusion. According to one election director, "County recorders were critical of the electoral process even before the NVRA was mandated. We try to minimize the problems, with redundant checks and numerous safeguards that reassure the general public. The internal integrity of the agency is on the line."[50]

Determining the impact of NVRA programs on voter registration and turnout, specifically for Latino communities, is therefore somewhat problematic.

STATEWIDE PERSPECTIVES

The Arizona Poll data source is a compilation of five statewide telephone surveys conducted with 2,625 adult residents of Arizona over the course of four years—1994, 1995, 1996, and 1997—by the Social Research Laboratory at Northern Arizona University. The polls offer Arizonans' responses pertaining to which methods of voter registration they were more likely to access to register to vote. According to self-reported data illustrated in table 4.1, the percentage of Arizonans registering to vote increased over the four-year polling cycle, from 72 percent in 1994 to 83 percent in 1997.[51] The largest rise in voter-registration rates, 9 percent, came in 1996. Because 1996 was a presidential election year, voter-registration rates were more likely to increase. However, the increase in voter registration remained well into 1997, which could possibly be attributed to the implementation of NVRA reform methods.

Table 4.1 Respondents Registered to Vote in Arizona							
	1994		1995		1996		1997	
	Frequency	%	Frequency	%	Frequency	%	Frequency	%
YES	429	72	458	74	436	83	331	83
NO	155	26	152	25	82	16	71	18
Don't Know	15	3	9	1	10	2	0	0
Total	600	101	619	100	527	101	402	101

Source: The Arizona Poll, February 1994 (600), February 1995 (619), February 1996 (527), and February 1997 (402).

Arizona residents were asked to self-identify with a particular race or ethnicity. One of the objectives of the study was to assess the effect of voter-registration reforms on Arizona's Latino population. With this in mind, Latino responses were extracted from the overall sample to evaluate the rate that Latino respondents registered to vote between 1994 and 1997. It is important to note that the Arizona Poll telephone surveys contain a very small number of Latino respondents. However, the figure presented on Latino respondents provides a glimpse into Latino voter registration rates.

According to table 4.2, voter-registration rates among Latino respondents varied over the four year polling cycle, from a low of 49 percent to a high of 81 percent. Latino respondents registering to vote declined from 77 percent in 1994 to 49 percent in 1995. However, the decline in Latino voter registration quickly turned around once the NVRA was implemented, rising to 73 percent in 1996 and 81 percent in 1997.

Arizona respondents were asked to indicate the process or method by which they actually registered to vote. Respondents indicated whether they registered

Table 4.2 Latino Respondents Registered to Vote in Arizona							
	1994		1995		1996		1997	
	Frequency	%	Frequency	%	Frequency	%	Frequency	%
YES	33	77	42	49	30	73	38	81
NO	10	23	41	49	10	24	9	19
Don't Know	0	0	2	2	1	2	0	0
Total	43	100	85	100	41	99	46	100

Source: The Arizona Poll, February 1994 (600), February 1995 (619), February 1996 (527), and February, 1997 (402).

through the traditional non-NVRA process (e.g., county clerk's/elections office, deputy registrar, or through a voter-registration drive), or through NVRA-type reform methods (e.g., mail-in registration or Arizona's modified motor-voter program).

Overall, Arizonans are more likely to register to vote using traditional methods of registration (40 percent) rather than reform methods of registration (28 percent). However, over the four-year polling cycle, Arizona respondents had a tendency to move away from non-NVRA methods of registration and toward NVRA-type reform methods.

As indicated in table 4.3, respondents registering to vote through more traditional methods of registration were more likely to register in person at the county clerk's/election office (18 percent) than through a voter-registration drive (16 percent). Fewer respondents registered via a deputy registrar (5 percent). Respondents registering to vote through reform methods of registration were more likely to register while applying for their driver's license (16 percent) than by mailing in their registration forms (12 percent). Almost one-third of the respondents (31 percent) could not remember how they registered to vote or had used a different method of registration. Respondents reported accessing other methods

Table 4.3 Methods of Voter Registration		
	Frequency	Percent
County Clerk/Elections Office	404	18
Deputy Registrars	119	5
Voter Registration Drive	345	16
Mail-in Ballots	262	12
Motor Vehicle Office	362	16
Don't Know	370	17
Other methods	339	14
Total	2201	100

Source: The Arizona Poll, February 1994 (429), October 1994 (399), February 1995 (458), October 1996 (584), February 1997 (331).

of voter registration such as registering through a high school, post office, public library, bank, local grocery store, community church, Headstart program, on-line, or upon becoming a U.S. citizen.

As suggested in figure 4.1, the likelihood of using NVRA-type registration methods more than non-NVRA registration methods is highly probable. NVRA-type registration is clearly increasing, whereas non-NVRA is declining. In 1994 almost two-thirds of the respondents (65 percent) reported that they were more likely to register through traditional methods than reform methods (35 percent).

Figure 4.1
Registration by NVRA-type and Non-NVRA Methods:
1994 to 1997

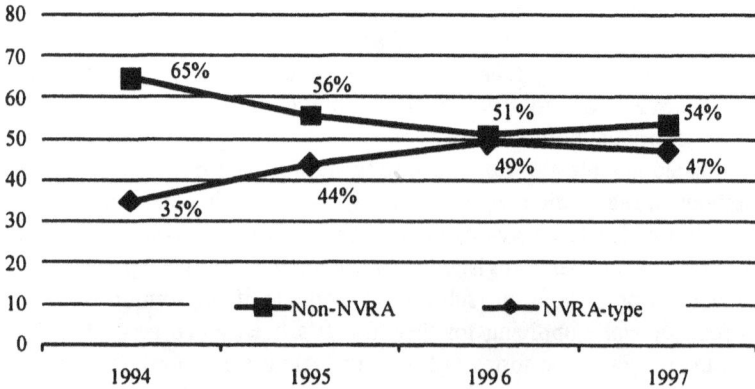

Source: The Arizona Poll, February 19914 (429), October 1994 (399), February 1995 (458), October 1996 (584), February 1997 (331).

Once voter-registration reforms were in place, the percentage of respondent registration rose to 44 percent in 1995 and 49 percent in 1996. In the 1996 presidential election year, Arizonans were almost equally divided between registering through traditional methods of registration (51 percent) and reform methods of registration (49 percent). In 1997, NVRA-type registration slipped slightly, to 47 percent. Overall NVRA-type registration increased 12 percentage points, while non-NVRA registration decreased 11 percentage points. Over time, Arizona respondents were more likely to register to vote using mail-in voter registration than at the county clerk's/election office. The percentage of Arizona residents registering through deputy registrars, voter-registration drives, and motor-voter programs remained fairly consistent over the four year polling period.

Table 4.4 indicates which registration method Arizona respondents utilized to register to vote. Between 1994 and 1997 the proportion of respondents registering through mail-in registration programs doubled, from 8 to 16 percent, whereas the proportion of respondents registering to vote through the county clerk's/election office decreased from 22 percent in 1994 to 16 percent in 1997.

At first glance, voter registration through voter-registration drives increased to 20 percent in 1996, then slipped to 15 percent in 1997, which is not totally unexpected because 1996 was a presidential-election year. In 1994, 15 percent of Arizona respondents reported registering through the MVD office, compared to 17 percent in 1995, 20 percent in 1996, and 16 percent in 1997.

When one takes into account that the sampling error could affect the results by 3 percentage points in either direction, respondents registering through MVD

Table 4.4 Methods of Voter Registration Reported by Respondents 1994 to 1997				
	1994	1995	1996	1997
Non-NVRA Registration Programs				
County Clerk/Elections Office	22%	17%	16%	16%
Deputy Registrars	6%	4%	5%	7%
Voter Registration Drive	15%	14%	20%	15%
NVRA Registration Programs				
Mail-in Ballots	8%	10%	17%	16%
Motor Vehicle Office	15%	17%	20%	16%
Public Assistance office	N/A	N/A	3%	1%
Don't Know	17%	18%	18%	17%
Other method of registration	17%	21%	1%	12%
Total	100	101%	100%	100%

Source: The Arizona Poll, February 1994 (429), October 1994 (399), February 1995 (459), October 1996 (441), February 1997 (331).

offices remained fairly consistent over the four year polling period. What accounts for the unvarying responses in motor-voter registration among Arizonans?

Once motor-voter was implemented, the Arizona Secretary of State's office reported a "substantial increase" in Arizona's voter registration rates.[52] Figure 4.2 indicates that prior to Arizona implementing motor-voter registration, voter-registration rates steadily declined 9 percentage points, from 66 percent in 1972 to 58 percent in 1976 and 57 percent in the 1980 presidential election. After implementation, state voter-registration rates increased significantly, to 66 percent in 1984 and 71 percent in both of the 1988 and 1992 presidential elections.

Arizona averaged a 12.2 percent[53] growth rate of voting-age population biennially during pre-motor-voter election years (1972–1982), and a 5.6 percent growth rate biennially during post-motor-voter election years (1984–1992).[54] In spite of experiencing a higher growth rate of potential voters in the pre-motor-voter years than the post-motor-voter years, only 57 percent of Arizona's potential electorate was registered to vote in 1980, compared to 71 percent in 1992.

Figure 4.2
Arizona Voter Registration for Presidential Elections:
1972 to 1992 Pre-Motor-Voter and Post-Motor-Voter Years

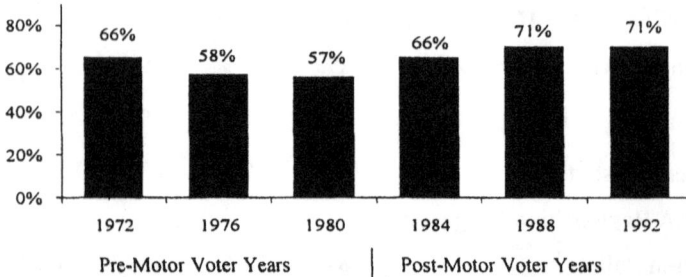

Pre-Motor Voter Years | Post-Motor Voter Years

Source: Crocker, 1994.

Arizona's off-year elections demonstrated a similar increase in registered voters. Figure 4.3 indicates that during Arizona's pre-motor-voter years, voter-registration rates declined from 60 percent in 1974 to 55 percent in 1978 and 1982. In post-motor-voter years, voter-registration rates in Arizona increased by 2 percent each off-election year, to 67 percent in 1986, 69 percent in 1990, and 71 percent in 1994. Again, more Arizonans, 71 percent, were registered to vote in 1992, compared to 57 percent in 1980.

According to the Arizona Secretary of State's office, the increase of voter-registration rates in post-motor-voter years "can be attributed to the accessibility of registering when conducting business at the Department of Motor Vehicles."[55]

Figure 4.3
Arizona Voter Registration for Off-Year Elections:
1974–1994 Pre-Motor-Voter and Post-Motor-Voter Years

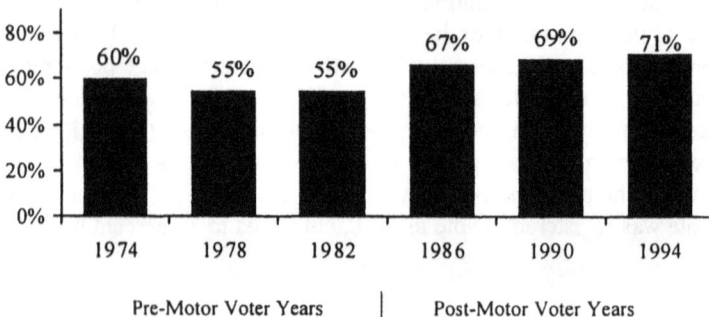

Pre-Motor Voter Years | Post-Motor Voter Years

Source: Crocker, 1994.

LATINOS AND NVRA-TYPE REFORMS

Voter-registration reforms such as the motor-voter program, agency-based registration, and mail-in registration were designed to target minorities and low-income and young people. Methods of registering to vote vary among the different socioeconomic populations (see Appendix G).

Race/ethnicity, income, and education are significant when it comes to selecting where or how Arizonans will register to vote, whereas age and party affiliation appear to have no significance. Latinos are less likely to benefit from NVRA-type reform methods of registration. Fewer Latinos (21 percent) than whites (30 percent) register through NVRA methods of registration. Only 8 percent of Latino respondents registered while obtaining their driver's license, compared to 18 percent of their white counterparts. However, more Latino respondents (13 percent) were likely to mail in their registration forms to a county clerk's/election office than were white respondents (12 percent). Voter-registration drives continue to be an effective method of registering Latinos (21 percent). Low-income Arizonans are less likely to benefit from NVRA reforms. Almost one-third (31 percent) of the registrants with income levels of $22,000 and more registered through the motor-voter or mail-in methods of registration, while less than one-fourth (23 percent) of the registrants with income levels below $22,000 registered through similar methods of registration. Low-income registrants were more likely to register to vote at the county clerk's/election office (22 percent) than to mail in their registration forms (8 percent) or register to vote while obtaining or renewing their driver's licenses (15 percent).

College graduates are more likely to benefit from NVRA reform methods of registration. More college graduates (31 percent) registered to vote through NVRA methods of registration than high school graduates (27 percent) and non-high-school graduates (22 percent). Respondents with less than a high school education (16 percent) were more likely to mail in their registration forms than individuals who graduated from high school (11 percent) or college (12 percent). Fewer non-high-school graduates (6 percent) than high school graduates (16 percent) and college graduates (19 percent) took advantage of motor-voter registration. More non-high-school graduates (24 percent) than high school graduates (21 percent) and college graduates (20 percent) were likely to have registered at the county clerk's/election office.

Age appears to have no significance when it comes to selecting where or how one will register to vote. More individuals between eighteen to twenty-nine years of age (18 percent) than those thirty years of age and older (15 percent) were likely to register while applying or renewing their driver's licenses. Fewer individuals between eighteen and twenty-nine (8 percent) than those thirty years old and older (9 percent) mailed in their registration forms to an election office. Individuals thirty years old and older (23 percent) were more likely to register through the county clerk's/election office than eighteen to twenty-nine year olds (16 percent). One in five individuals eighteen to twenty-nine years of age reported registering at other places, more likely through their local high schools, on college campuses, or through their workplaces.

Party identification also appears to have little significance when people decide where or how to register to vote. Motor-voter registration was greatest among Independents (20 percent) but not significantly higher than for Republicans (17 percent) and Democrats (15 percent). Similarly, mail-in registration among the different party affiliations—Independents (13 percent), Republicans and Democrats (12 percent)—was closely related. The analysis between Arizona registrants' methods of voter registration and demographic groupings suggests that race/ethnicity, income, and education are significant when deciding where or how Arizonans will register to vote, whereas age and party affiliation did not appear to have any significance.

Liberalized methods of registration such as mail-in registration and motor-voter registration are often suggested as possible solutions to dismal election turnout rates. Reformed methods of registration, however, do not guarantee that individuals will actually turn out on election day to cast their ballots.

NVRA-TYPE METHODS AND VOTER TURNOUT

What is the likelihood that individuals registering through reform (NVRA-type) methods of voter registration actually turn out to vote on election day? Table 4.5 indicates that the relationship between Arizonans registering through reform (NVRA-type) methods and traditional (non-NVRA) registrants and those individuals who actually voted in the 1992 presidential election is statistically significant. The cutoff criterion for statistical significance is .05. The chi square test of significance between the two variables is .006, well below the .05 cutoff. The analysis shows that there is a relationship between NVRA-type and non-NVRA registrants and casting a vote in the 1992 presidential election. Individuals registering through traditional (non-NVRA) methods of registration (95 percent) were more likely to vote in the 1992 presidential election than individuals who registered through reform (NVRA-type) methods (90 percent). Even though the relationship is statistically significant, the lambda is only .09, which indicates a weak relationship between the two variables.

Table 4.5
NVRA-Type and Non-NVRA Registrants Voting in the 1992 Presidential Election

Voted in the 1992 Election	NVRA-type Registration	Non-NVRA Registration
Yes		
Count	385	511
Col. Pct	90%	95%
No		
Count	42	28
Col. Pct	10%	5%
Column	427	539
Total	44%	56%

CHI SQUARED	DF	SIGNIFICANCE
7.636	1	0.006

CELLS WITH EF < 5	LAMBDA
NONE	.094

Sources: The Arizona Poll, February 1995 and   October 1996 (Registrants 966).

Table 4.6 illustrates the relationship between NVRA-type and non-NVRA registrants and reported voting in the 1994 general election is statistically significant. Using the .05 cutoff, the chi square test of significance (.002) is well below the level of significance. More non-NVRA registrants (81 percent) than NVRA-type registrants (71 percent) reported that they cast a vote in the 1994 general election. The analysis shows that there is a statistically significant relationship between the two variables. However, the magnitude of the association is .076, indicating a weak relationship. The analysis conducted between reform (NVRA-type) methods and traditional (non-NVRA) methods and reported voting in the 1992 presidential election and the 1994 general election suggests that the two variables are related. However, the analysis also concludes that the relationship between NVRA-type and non-NVRA methods of registration and voter turnout in the 1992 and 1994 elections is minimal.

Table 4.6
NVRA-Type and Non-NVRA Registrants
Voting in the 1994 General Election

Voted in the 1994 Election	NVRA-type Registration	Non-NVRA Registration
Yes		
Count	229	301
Col Pct	71%	81%
No		
Count	96	73
Col Pct	30%	20%
Column	325	374
Total	47%	54%

CHI SQUARED	DF	SIGNIFICANCE
9.523	1	0.002

CELLS WITH EF < 5	LAMBDA
NONE	.076

Sources: The Arizona Poll, February 1995 and October 1996
(Registrants 966).

NOTES

1. Election director, personal interview by Elaine Rodriquez, June 18, 1996.
2. Public-assistance program regional manager, personal interview by Elaine Rodriquez, July 26, 1996.
3. Election director, personal interview, June 18, 1996.
4. Ibid. [The same page as the preceding note]
5. Election director, personal interview, June 18, 1996.
6. A fax-transmitted questionnaire was sent to all Arizona County recorders. Nine of fifteen county recorders (a response rate of 60 percent) responded to a fifteen-question survey. The survey was faxed and returned between July and August of 1996.
7. Individuals who apply for agency services have the option of either registering to vote or declining to register to vote. If the applicant decides not to register then the individual must sign a declination attesting that they did not wish to register.
8. Arizona, Secretary of State, *Reporting Requirements Under the NVRA* (1995), Phoenix, Arizona.
9. Ibid. [The same page as the preceding note]
10. Arizona, Secretary of State, *Task Force Report: National Voter Registration Act of 1993* (1994), p. 2.
11. Election director, personal interview, June 18, 1996.
12. Arizona, Secretary of State, *Offer of Voter Registration*, Form NVRA-5 (1994).
13. Election director, personal interview by Elaine Rodriquez, June 17, 1996.
14. Ibid. [The same page as the preceding note]
15. County recorder, personal interview by Elaine Rodriquez, June 17, 1996.
16. Public-assistance program regional manager, personal interview, July 26, 1996.
17. Executive director, telephone interview by Elaine Rodriquez, March 10, 1997.
18. Ibid. [The same page as the preceding note]
19. Executive director, telephone interview, March 10, 1997.
20. Ibid. [The same page as the preceding note]
21. Election director, personal interview by Elaine Rodriquez, June 17, 1996.
22. Election director, personal interview, June 18, 1996.
23. County recorder, personal interview, June 17, 1996.
24. Election director, personal interview, June 18, 1996.
25. Election director, personal interview, June 18, 1996; county recorder, personal interview, June 17, 1996; and election director, personal interview, June 17, 1996.
26. Public-assistance program regional manager, personal interview, July 26, 1996; and public-assistance program regional manager, personal interview, July 25, 1996.
27. Public-assistance program regional manager, personal interview, July 25, 1996.
28. Public-assistance program regional manager, personal interview by Elaine Rodriquez, July 26, 1996.
29. Ibid. [The same page as the preceding note]
30. Public-assistance program regional manager, personal interview, July 25, 1996; and public-assistance program regional manager, personal interview by Elaine Rodriquez, July 26, 1996.
31. Ibid. [The same page as the preceding note]

32. Public-assistance program regional manager, personal interview, July 25, 1996.

33. Public-assistance program regional manager, personal interview, July 26, 1996; public-assistance program regional manager, personal interview, July 25, 1996; and public-assistance program regional manager, personal interview by Elaine Rodriquez, July 26, 1996.

34. Public-assistance program regional manager, personal interview, July 25, 1996.

35. Public-assistance program regional manager, personal interview, July 25, 1996; and public-assistance program regional manager, personal interview, July 26, 1996.

36. Ibid. [The same page as the preceding note]

37. Public-assistance program regional manager, personal interview, July 26, 1996.

38. Ibid. [The same page as the preceding note]

39. Ibid. [The same page as the preceding note]

40. Public-assistance program regional manager, personal interview, July 25, 1996.

41. Ibid. [The same page as the preceding note]

42. Council of State Governments, *The National Voter Registration Act of 1993 Manual* (KY: Lexington, 1994), p. 33.

43. Election director, personal interview, June 18, 1996; County recorder, personal interview, June 17, 1996.

44. County recorder, personal interview, June 17, 1996.

45. Election director, personal interview, June 18, 1996.

46. Public-assistance program regional manager, personal interview, July 25, 1996.

47. Ibid. [The same page as the preceding note]

48. Public-assistance program regional manager, personal interview, July 26, 1996.

49. Ibid. [The same page as the preceding note]

50. Election director, personal interview, June 18, 1996.

51. The 1994 Arizona Poll was conducted between February 22 and February 29, 1994. A random sample of 600 Arizona residents was interviewed by telephone. The 1995 Arizona Poll was conducted between February 20 and February 24, 1995. A random sample of 619 Arizona residents was interviewed by telephone. The 1996 Arizona Poll was conducted between February 26 and February 29, 1996. A random sample of 528 Arizona residents was interviewed by telephone. Figures in each of these sampling sizes were subject to a sampling error estimated at plus or minus 3 percent. The results based on this sample size are estimated to have a 95 percent confidence level. The 1997 Arizona Poll was conducted between February 24 and February 27, 1997. A random sample of 402 Arizona residents was interviewed by telephone. Figures in this sampling size are subject to a sampling error estimated at plus or minus 4 percent. The results based on this sample size are estimated to have a 95 percent confidence level.

52. Arizona Secretary of State, "Research Figures for Motor Voter" (1991),   p. 1.

53. The average percentage growth increase for pre-motor voter years (1972-1982) is 73.2/6 general elections = 12.2% biennially. The average percentage growth increase for post-motor voter years (1984-1992) is 28.2/5 general elections = 5.64% biennially.

54. Royce Crocker, *Voter Registration and Turnout for Each State: 1948-1992* (Washington D.C.: Congressional Research Service, Library of Congress, 1994), p. 70.

55. Arizona Secretary of State, "Research Figures for Motor Voter" (1991),   pp. 1–2.

CHAPTER FIVE

CONCLUSION: NVRA AS AN ELECTION-REFORM STRATEGY

> NVRA has made voter registration available to a whole lot of groups. They now are only disenfranchised because they choose not to participate.
> ⁓Arizona election director⁓

The National Voter Registration Act of 1993 (NVRA) was designed to create a government initiated voter registration system that shifts the burden of registering to vote from the citizen to the government by offering eligible citizens additional and less cumbersome opportunities to register to vote. The objective of NVRA was to increase the number of registered voters and voter turnout in the United States.

This chapter looks at the effectiveness of NVRA and its consequences for Latino communities. It addresses the following questions: 1) Which NVRA-type methods are most effective? 2) Who is taking advantage of NVRA? and 3) How successful have NVRA-type reforms been?

NVRA REFORMS IN ARIZONA

Overall, the National Voter Registration Act has been somewhat successful in achieving its intended objectives. NVRA succeeded in increasing the total number of voter-registration applications in Arizona. The likelihood of Arizonans making use of NVRA-type reforms, such as mail-in and motor-voter, is highly probable. Once Arizona initiated NVRA-type measures in 1992, voter registration remained consistent, even though voter turnout plummeted in the following elections. This decline was not unprecedented. In the 1968 and 1972 elections, voter registration rose and voter turnout fell because new voters—citizens between the ages of eighteen and twenty-one—were enfranchised.[1]

Over the four year polling cycle from 1994 to 1997, Arizona's general population had a tendency to move away from non-NVRA methods of registration— e.g., through a county clerk's/elections office, deputy registrar, or voter-registration drive—and toward NVRA-type methods of registration (e.g., mail-in registration or motor-voter program). The number of Arizonans registering by means of NVRA-type methods climbed 12 percentage points, while registration via non-NVRA-type methods dropped 11 percentage points. Moreover, this study found that individuals registering through NVRA-type methods were less likely to vote in the 1992 general election (5 percent) and 1994 general election (10 percent) than individuals registering through non-NVRA methods.

The reported impact of the NVRA in Arizona by the Secretary of State's office reinforces many of the findings presented in this study. Arizona's Secretary of State office reported that more than three-fourths (77 percent) of Arizona's voter registration applications were processed through NVRA methods, whereas only about one-fifth (21 percent) of the applications were processed through non-NVRA methods for the 1996/1998 and 1998/2000 reporting periods.[2] Arizona processed twice as many voter-registration applications and new valid registrations in the 1998/2000 period compared to the 1996/1998 period.[3] Of the new registrants, 12,258 (or 2.6 percent) in the 1996/1998 reporting period and 37,331 (or 4.1 percent) for the 1998/2000 reporting period were duplicate applications. Between the two reporting periods, mail-in registration rose from 51 percent to 54 percent, whereas motor-voter registration declined from 19 percent to 17 percent. Individuals registering through non-NVRA methods remained fairly consistent (20 percent and 19 percent, respectively), while registration through other agencies (i.e., disabilities agencies, armed services, and state-designated agencies) rose from 3 percent to 6 percent between the 1996/1998 and 1998/2000 reporting periods. Arizona's county clerk's/election offices deleted 219,986 (9 percent) and 189,232 (7 percent) statewide registrants from the voter-registration lists over the two reporting periods.[4]

The decline in motor-voter registration may be attributed to the fact that Arizona's Motor Vehicle Division (MVD) moved to a forty-four-year driver's license renewal period, whereby a driver's license is valid from the time an individual is sixteen years old until he or she turns sixty.[5] Once an individual has been issued a driver's license, she does not have to renew the license unless she changes her name, loses her license, moves, or the license is revoked; and renewal can be done through the mail.[6] This inadvertently makes the motor-voter registration program less effective. Arizona is the only state with this kind of a renewal cycle.[7]

Arizona's motor-voter program had some effect on voter registration for presidential and midterm election years. Pre-motor-voter election years demonstrated a decline in voter registration, compared to a post-motor-voter election increase.

LATINOS AND TWO-TIERED PLURALISM

Arizona's Latino population, like the U.S. Latino Population, nearly quadrupled between 1970 and 2000, ranking the state fourth among states in Latino population. Latinos are the largest ethnic group in the United States. Much of this increase can be attributed to "ongoing in-migration."[8]

Understanding the role Latino communities play in American politics is central to questions regarding the effectiveness of NVRA. Models such as group theory or pluralism (David Truman and Robert Dahl)[9], coalition bias (Clarence Stone)[10], and internal colonialism (Mario Barrerra)[11] have been used to explain the Latino political experience within the context of American politics, but each model presents problems when applied to Latinos because the models treat all

Latinos as a homogeneous group, not recognizing historical, structural, socioe-conomic, racial, and ethnic differences.[12]

Group theory or pluralism suggests that public policy is the result of various competing interests. Collectively, individuals utilize their available resources to gain access to the political system, and through the bargaining process (lobby-ing) can influence policy outcomes. However, in order to influence policy out-comes, groups must gain access to the "policy arena," which requires an abundance of resources. According to pluralist thought, group resources are noncumulative; that is, they are dispersed among various groups, and no one group accumulates all the power resources. All groups thus compete at the same level. Critics of pluralist thought argue that groups who are deficient or plentiful in one resource area are more than likely to be deficient or plentiful in other re-source areas. Furthermore, opponents disparage the pluralist model as ahistorical in that it treats all racial and ethnic groups the same, not taking into considera-tion each group's specific circumstances.[13]

Rodney Hero's two-tiered pluralism suggests that because of historical, so-cioeconomic, and other structural factors, Latinos "have largely been relegated to a lower social and political standing" within the policy arena,[14] resulting in low civic participation, under-representation in appointed and elected positions, and the lack of practical policies that would advance their well-being. According to Hero, the Latino political experience in the Southwest parallels the African American political experience in the South. He concludes that the Latino strug-gle has evolved from "de jure exclusion, to de facto segregation, to de jure plu-ralism."[15] Latino political struggle   is exemplified by de jure exclusionary policies, such as drawing the white line   and granting the franchise only to white, male citizens, to de facto segregationist practices, such as creating Mex-ican-only schools and public accommodations, to de jure pluralism or desegre-gation politics established in the *Mendez*,[16] the *Delgado*,[17] and the *Brown* court decisions, and voting-rights legislation and affirmative-action policy.[18]

The shadow of conquest defines Mexican American's political power with-in the context of the American political system, whereas the Mexican communi-ty, by reason of noncitizenship status, is restricted from the political process. Together, these communities struggle to gain social, economic, and political equity.

Today, Latinos contend with de facto segregation, as is characterized by educational and economic inequality. Because of the continued in-migration, Latinos are forced to contend with de jure segregation such as anti-immigration and anti-language legislation targeted at language minorities, which for the general population equate to all Latinos. These policies are not designed to promote Latinos' social, political, or economic interests but rather create a climate that places the Latino community under attack.

Measures such as Proposition 63 (1986),[19] Proposition 187 (1994),[20] Proposition 209 (1996), and Proposition 227 (1998)[21] launched an anti-Latino sentiment that migrated from California to other Western and Southwestern states, such as Washington, Oregon, Utah, Arizona, and Colorado. Arizona followed California's lead. In 1988, Proposition 106 was adopted as a constitutional amendment, considered by some to be the most restrictive English-only law to date.[22] In 1999, Arizona's Supreme Court ruled the English-only law to be unconstitutional.[23] Less restrictive English-only laws have passed in twenty-four states,[24] and fourteen states have considered similar bills.

In 1995, Arizonans failed to pass a measure similar to California's Proposition 187. However, that same year legislation passed which denies access to preschool programs (e.g., the Family Literacy Program) by individuals who are not legal residents, making it Arizona's first law restricting educational services to undocumented residents. In 1996 the passage of welfare-reform and immigration-reform bills restricted government programs and public assistance to immigrants, documented or undocumented. In the 2000 presidential election, voters in Arizona passed Proposition 203, English for the Children, ending bilingual education programs in Arizona.[25] A similar proposal did not make it onto Colorado's ballot because the Supreme Court ruled that the ballot title was "misleading."[26] However, Utah voters passed an English-only initiative.[27]

After the passage of California's antiaffirmative measure, proponents targeted Arizona, Colorado, Oregon, and Washington as potential states to pass additional antiaffirmative-action legislation.[28] Other evidence of attack is the *Shaw* decision (1993) challenging majority-minority redistricting of alternating districts. This decision affects the redrawing of districts after the 2000 reapportionments schematics and impacts this decade's presidential and midterm elections.

These public policies are a reaction to the growing Latino population and force public officials to take notice and respond, either supportively or unkindly, to Latino interests. Elected officials are less likely to court nonvoters and less responsive via government policies aimed at the nonvoting community interests. Often elected officials' policy response to Latino communities is driven by "race and ethnic determinates," which consequently produce public policy that provides either "protection for Latinos" or "special programs" designed to promote Latino status. Both types of policy responses are "symbolic or purchased" pluralism, and are reactionary in nature.[29] Creating "symbolic" or "purchased" pluralism, such as the Voting Rights Act and, more recently, NVRA, are seen as compensating Latinos for past electoral practices of exclusion.

NVRA AND THE DISENFRANCHISED

The National Voter Registration Act of 1993 is considered the most progressive electoral reform since the Voter Rights Act of 1965. NVRA was designed to equalize" the political playing field by making the electoral process less cumbersome so that disenfranchised groups could achieve more than marginal inclusion. But NVRA-type reforms have been less advantageous to disenfranchised populations such as Latinos, the poor, and less-educated individuals. Enfranchised populations such as whites, upper-income individuals and families, and college graduates were much more likely to utilize NVRA-type reforms as a means of registering to vote. Latinos were less likely to register via mail-in ballots (13 percent) and MVD offices (8 percent) and were much more likely to register through non-NVRA methods such as the county clerk/election offices (21 percent), voter-registration drives (21 percent), or through other sources (20 percent) such as high school, the post office, the public library, a community church, Headstart, or upon becoming a U.S. citizen. Much of the increase in Latino voter registration in Arizona can be attributed to voter-registration drives conducted by Latino special-interest groups.

These findings are supported by a study conducted by Raymond E. Wolfinger and Jonathan Hoffman (2001) using data sources from the 1996 Voter Supplement of the U.S. Census Bureau's Current Population Survey (CPS) to determine who used NVRA methods to register to vote and whether they were more likely to turn out in the first NVRA election. Wolfinger and Hoffman found that aggregate voter registration had declined slightly from the 1992 (78 percent) to 1996 (77 percent) elections. Some individuals did register through NVRA methods (DMVs and public agencies).[30] A little more than one-fifth (22 percent) of the Latinos registered between January 1, 1995, and the 1996 presidential election. When Wolfinger and Hoffman controlled for all demographic variables in their study, they found that Latinos were 4 percent more likely to be new registrants.[31]

Regarding which citizens were likely to use NVRA methods, Wolfinger and Hoffman found that mobile residents were much more likely to take advantage of the NVRA.[32] New Latino registrants (21 percent) were less likely than whites (32 percent), African Americans (23 percent), and Asian Americans (29 percent) to register at DMVs. Latino registrants (6 percent) were a little more likely than white registrants (3 percent), and less likely than African Americans (7 percent), to register at public-assistance agencies.[33]

According to Wolfinger and Hoffman, "gaps remained between minorities and Whites in the use of the NVRA with a greater difference for Latinos than African Americans."[34] Even when demographic differences are controlled for, "new Latino and African American registrants were less likely than their White counterparts to take advantage of the NVRA."[35] Furthermore, Wolfinger and Hoffman found that public assistance agency registrants (14 percent) and MVDs' registrants (9 percent) were less likely to vote in 1996 than other new registrants.[36] Wolfinger and Hoffman's findings, and the findings presented in the previous chapters, suggest that perhaps NVRA-designated agencies such as DMVs or public-assistance offices may not be the most effective agencies to register Latino populations, since Latinos may be less likely to frequent those agencies.

Over time, NVRA may assist Latinos to gain political inclusion. However, the expectation that NVRA independently would lead to increases in the number of Latino registrants finds that such policies will not equalize Latinos' political standing. One must be reminded that NVRA is an election-reform strategy only for the citizen population. The high percentage of Latino noncitizens among the

U.S. Latino population and more specifically Arizona's Latino population is a major factor contributing to low Latino voter turnout rates. For new Latino immigrants to become integrated into the American political process they must first become naturalized citizens. Recently, policy initiatives that would increase the numbers of naturalized Latino citizens were introduced to reduce the backlog of naturalization cases. In addition, several Central and South American countries initiated dual-naturalization policies whereby immigrants can secure U.S. citizenship without losing social, economic, and political rights in their countries of origin.[37]

As discussed in a previous chapter, Latino voter participation varies considerably from state to state and within enclaves in particular states. For example, New Mexico's Hispanos and especially Northern New Mexico Hispanos or Miami Cubanos demonstrate high-levels of political participation. Such socioeconomic factors as age, generation, and education affect voter-turnout levels among both the general Latino population and Arizona's Latino population. Also, Latinos may lack a clear understanding of the political process, the significance of voting and not voting, and its consequences. According to one county recorder, Latinos don't make the connection between politicians' decisions and how those decisions will affect their community: the jobs, the roads, the schools, and the parks that will or won't result.[38] Lastly, Latinos have a misconception that if they register to vote and then do vote they necessarily will get called for jury duty.[39]

Nationally, Latinos have made political gains at the voting booth. Between the last two presidential elections, Latino voter turnout increased by 1.6 million voters. Much of the increase in Latino voter turnout parallels Latino population increases in the ten most populated states, ranging from a high in Nevada with an increase of 38 percent to a low in Colorado with only a 4 percent increase. Arizona's Latino voter turnout increased by 49,000 voters, or 17 percent. Continued increases in Latino voting ultimately can sway presidential elections.

NVRA AS AN ELECTION-REFORM STRATEGY

In the early 1990s, Arizona scrambled to pass several pre-NVRA measures in an effort to be included among the few states exempted from NVRA. However, taking the lead and liberalizing state voter registration laws did not rescue Arizona from having to amend voter-registration procedures to comply.

Initially, Arizona's public officials regarded NVRA—an unfunded mandate—as an infringement on the state's right to manage its own election process. Nonetheless, the majority of county recorders and election directors felt that NVRA has been successful in achieving its objectives. Public assistance agency managers, however, feel that mandated agency voter registration has created animosity and has not had a significant impact on increasing voter participation. According to one agency manager, "If they have to agree to something to get those checks, they are going to do it, and take it home and throw it in the garbage."[40] Other managers believe that noncitizens and undocumented applicants seeking emergency services might be too intimidated to apply for services if registering to vote is strongly promoted, especially if the way it is enforced implies the involvement of a governmental authority or "police action."[41]

Once NVRA was implemented, county recorders, election directors, and public-assistance mangers expressed dissatisfaction with the policy. Much of the dissatisfaction has been associated with 1, the costs of implementing the new voter registration programs, 2, the record maintenance required by the NVRA, and 3, the cooperation and efficiency of other governmental agencies who are required by NVRA to offer voter-registration services.

State and county respondents have provided recommendations they feel would ease some of the complexities of NVRA reporting requirements and aid in developing intra-agency and inter-agency competence in the implementation. Following are the recommendations:

1. Provide additional training for MVD and public agency staff emphasizing the legal requirements of NVRA. Focus the training on the proper voter registration instructions to pass on to their clientele, and how to correctly process and submit voter-registration applications.
2. Create one application for both MVD and voter registration that can be easily detached and forwarded to the county recorder's office.
3. Eliminate the declination form requirement.
4. Purchase new computer systems and software adequate for file maintenance.
5. Obtain a reduced postal rate for all NVRA-related items.

Ultimately, county and state managers and administrators believe that NVRA will work only if the people who implement the program are willing to make a concerted effort to make it work. Their attitudes—passive or proactive—will determine the success of NVRA.

IMPLICATIONS FOR THE LATINO COMMUNITY

The fact that Latinos were referred to by scholars as "forgotten people"[42] or "forgotten Americans"[43] for many decades in the 20th century illustrates not only their political exclusion but also their alienation from the mainstream of American life. Given such a prolonged state of legalized social and political exclusion, it is to be expected that, even as legal barriers fade away, there will be a time lag before Latinos achieve great political integration.

Latinos continue to cope with de facto segregation and are forced to contend with de jure exclusionary policies aimed at both generational Hispanos and new Latino immigrants. However, Rodney Hero's bleak view of two-tiered pluralism fails to take into account the essence of Latino political power, which lies in the ethnic enclaves of individual states. In fact, Latino communities are in a unique position to seize political clout. First, the growing numbers of new and old Latino families in strategic electoral states collectively amass a significant proportion of the states' population. Second, the relatively young Latino segment in search of community reassurance, and the ever-increasing noncitizen population encountering exclusive institutions, want to be embraced and provided with the political resources to become a voice for Latino community interests. Finally, traditional community-based, grass-roots mobilization conducted by Latino special-interest groups utilizing NVRA mail-in voter-registration methods is a much more effective voter-registration strategy for Latino communities.

Over time, government-mandated policies like NVRA may allow for Latinos to inch their way into the economic, social, and political institutions, but government-sponsored programs themselves will not equalize the playing field for Latinos. The Latino community—old and new—collectively will redefine how the game of politics is played.

NOTES

1. Federal Election Commission, "The Impact of the National Voter Registration Act of 1993 on the Administration of Federal Elections," June 1997, retrieved July 27, 2000, from the Elections and Voting database on the World Wide Web: http://www.fec.gov/votregis/nvrasum.htm.

2. Arizona Secretary of State, *NVRA Reporting Form 1998* (Phoenix, Arizona, 1999), p. 2; and Arizona Secretary of State, *NVRA Reporting Form 2000* (Phoenix, Arizona, 2001), p. 3.

3. Between the 1996/1998 federal election cycle, Arizona processed 469,826 voter-registration applications. Almost one-half (230,834) were new valid registrations. Between the 1998/2000 federal election cycle, Arizona processed 882,345 voter registration applications. Less than one-half (407,473) of these were new valid registrations.

4. Arizona Secretary of State, *NVRA Reporting Form 1998* (Phoenix, Arizona, 1999), pp. 1–15; *NVRA Reporting Form 2000* (Phoenix, Arizona, 2001), pp. 1–20.

5. Arizona State Senate, Committee on Transportation, *S. B. 1295—Driver's License: Omnibus Revisions* (Phoenix, Arizona, 1993), pp. 6–9.

6. American Association of Motor Vehicle Administrators, "Administration, Terms, and Age Requirements for State Driver Licenses," January 1, 1996, pp. 1–2.

7. Ibid., p. 2.

8. Tony Affigne, 2000. "Latino Politics in the United States: An Introduction," *Political Science & Politics* Vol. 33, no. 3 (September 2000), p. 525.

9. Rodney E. Hero, *Latinos and the U.S. Political System* (Philadelphia, Temple University Press, 1992), pp. 12–15.

10. Ibid., pp. 15–16.

11. Ibid., pp. 17–18.

12. Rodney E. Hero, *Latinos and the U.S. Political System* (Philadelphia, Temple University Press, 1992), pp.18–29; and "Questions and Approaches in Understanding Latino Politics: The Need for Clarification and Bridging," *National Political Science Review* 3 (1993), pp. 153–157.

13. Rodney E. Hero, *Latinos and the U.S. Political System* (Philadelphia, Temple University Press, 1992), pp.18–19.

14. Ibid., p. 29.

15. Rodney E. Hero, *Latinos and the U.S. Political System* (Philadelphia: Temple University Press, 1992), p. 192.

16. In *Mendez et al v. Westminister School District of Orange County* (1946), U.S. District Court ruled that "segregation was illegal because it was not required by [California] state law and because there was no valid educational justification for segregation." See in Joel Spring, *Deculturalization and the Struggle for Equality* (New York: McGraw-Hill, Inc., 2001), p. 108.

17. In *Delgado v. Bastrop Independent School District* (1948), a Texas Court ruled that "segregating Mexican American children was illegal and discriminatory," thus requiring an end to segregation within the school district. See in Joel Spring, *Deculturalization and the Struggle for Equality*, p. 108.

18. Rodney E. Hero, *Latinos and the U.S. Political System* (Philadelphia: Temple University Press, 1992), p. 192.

19. Proposition 63 (1986) is an English-only initiative. See in R. Reese, "Language Diversity and the Politics of the English Only Movement in the U.S.," paper presented at the 34th World Congress of the International Institute of Sociology, Tel Aviv, Israel, 10 July 1999, http://www.csupomona.edu, p. 5.

20. Proposition 187 (1994) denying health benefits, education, and social services to illegal immigrants passed in California. Proposition 187 was ruled unconstitutional in 1997.

21. Proposition 209 (1996) ending state-supported affirmative action practices in state government and education institutions, and Proposition 227 (1998) ending bilingual education in public schools. See Holly Yeager, "Prop. 209 Proponent Takes His Campaign to the Nation, *"Latino Link on the Web*, 3 August 1997, http://www. latinolink.com/news.htm.

22. R. Reese, "Language Diversity and the Politics of the English Only Movement in the U.S.," p. 5.

23. "Arizona's English-only Law Ruled Unconstitutional," *CNN on the Web*, 29 April 1998, http:// www.cnn.com.

24. English-only laws have passed in Alabama, Alaska, Arizona (ruled unconstitutional in 1999), Arkansas, California, Colorado, Florida, Georgia, Hawaii (a bilingual state), Illinois (repealed in 1991), Indiana, Kentucky, Mississippi, Missouri, Montana, Nebraska, New Hampshire, North Carolina, North Dakota, South Carolina, South Dakota, Tennessee, Virginia, and Wyoming. See Anthony Collings, "Rejection Seen for English-only Measure," *CNN on the Web*, 4 December 1996, http://coloquio.com/english/cnneng. html.

25. Betsey Bayless, "2000 General Election Ballot Measures," *Arizona Secretary of State on the Web*, 3 August 2000, http:// www.sosaz.com/election/general/2000/ ballotmeasures.htm.

26. "Bilingual Foes Grid for Ballot," *The Daily Sentinel*, 10 September 2000, 1A.

27. "2000 Election Ballot Measure Results," *Ballot Watch on the Web*, 10 November 2000, http://www.ballotwatch.org.

28. R. Reese, "Language Diversity and the Politics of the English Only Movement in the U.S.," p. 8–9.

29. Rodney E. Hero, *Latinos and the U.S. Political System* (Philadelphia: Temple University Press, 1992), p. 192.

30. Wolfinger and Hoffman stated that 15 percent of the new registrants registered for the 1996 presidential election after January 1, 1995. See Raymond E. Wolfinger and Jonathan Hoffman, "Registering and Voting with Motor Voter," *Political Science & Politics*, no.1 (March 2001), pp. 85–86.

31. Raymond E. Wolfinger and Jonathan Hoffman, "Registering and Voting with Motor Voter," *Political Science & Politics*, no.1 (March 2001), pp. 85–86.

32. Ibid., p. 86.

33. Ibid., p. 87.

34. Ibid., p. 88.

35. Ibid., p. 90.

36. Ibid., p. 89.

37. Christine Marie Sierra, Teresa Carrillo, Louis DeSipio, and Michael Jones-Correa, "Latino Immigration and Citizenship," *Political Science & Politics* Vol. 33, no. 3 (September, 2000), p. 538.

38. County recorder, personal nterview by Elaine Rodriquez, June 17, 1996.

39. Election director, personal interview by Elaine Rodriquez, June 18, 1996; County recorder, personal interview, June 17, 1996.

40. Public assistance program manager, personal interview by Elaine Rodriquez, July 25, 1996.

41. Ibid. [The same page as the preceding note]

42. George I. Sanchez, *Forgotten People* (New Mexico: Calvin Horn Publisher, Inc., 1967), p. 98.

43. Julian Samora, ed., *La Raza: Forgotten Americans* (Notre Dame: University of Notre Dame Press, 1966), pp. 201–211.

APPENDIX A

International Ranking of Voter Turnout, 1945 to 2001, and Election Procedures

Country	Average Voter Turnout Voter	Number of Elections	Compulsory Voting Laws	Compulsory Registration	Type of Registration
Italy	92.0	15	Yes	Yes	Voter-L
Iceland	89.3	17	No	No	National-L
Portugal	88.2	10	No	Yes	Voters-L
New Zealand	86.0	19	No	Yes	No Data
Belgium	84.8	18	Yes	Yes	National-L
Austria	84.4	17	Yes	Yes	National-L
Australia	84.2	22	Yes	Yes	Voters-L/M/DD/DM/I/ME
Sweden	84.1	17	No	Yes	National-L
Netherlands	83.8	16	Yes	Yes	Voter-L
Denmark	83.6	22	No	Yes	National-L
Mauritius	82.4	7	No	No	Voters-DD
Canada	82.6	18	No	No	Voters-L/M/DM/I
Greece	80.8	18	Yes	Yes	No Data
Israel	80.3	15	No	Yes	No Data
Germany	80.2	14	No	Yes	Voters-M/O
Norway	79.2	15	No	Yes	National-L
Malta	78.9	14	No	No	No Data
Finland	78.1	16	No	Yes	National-L
Spain	76.4	8	No	Yes	National-L, O
Ireland	74.9	16	No	No	National-M/A/DD
United Kingdom	73.8	16	No	Yes	Voters-M
Papua New Guinea	72.2	8	No	Yes	Voters-M

APPENDIX A--CONTINUED

International Ranking of Voter Turnout, 1945 to 2001, and Election Procedures

Country	Average Voter Turnout Voter	Number of Elections	Compulsory Voting Laws	Compulsory Registration	Type of Registration
Japan	68.7	22	No	Yes	Voters-L
Costa Rica	68.1	13	Yes	Yes	Voters-DD/O
Venezuela	67.2	11	No	No	Other-Voters
France	67.3	15	Yes	No	Voters
Trinidad & Tobago	66.5	12	No	No	No Data
Barbados	63.9	11	No	No	Voters-DD
Luxembourg	63.5	13	Yes	Yes	No Data
Bahamas	63.4	6	No	Yes	Voters
India	61.5	13	No	Yes	Voters-DD
Jamaica	58.6	12	No	No	No Data
Switzerland	51.9	14	Yes	Yes	National-L
United States	47.7	28	No	No	Voters
Botswana	46.2	7	No	No	Voters-L/O
Columbia	36.2	20	Yes	Yes	Voters-L

Source: International Institute for Democracy and Electoral Assistance, 2002; aceproject.org, 2007; United States (excluding election-day registration states: Maine, Minnesota, Oregon, Wisconsin and North Dakota). Type of Registration (L=Links, M=Mail, DD=Door-to-Door, DM=Data Matching, I=Internet, O=Other.

APPENDIX B

Voter Turnout Among Whites, African Americans, and Latinos in Presidential Elections: 1972 to 2004

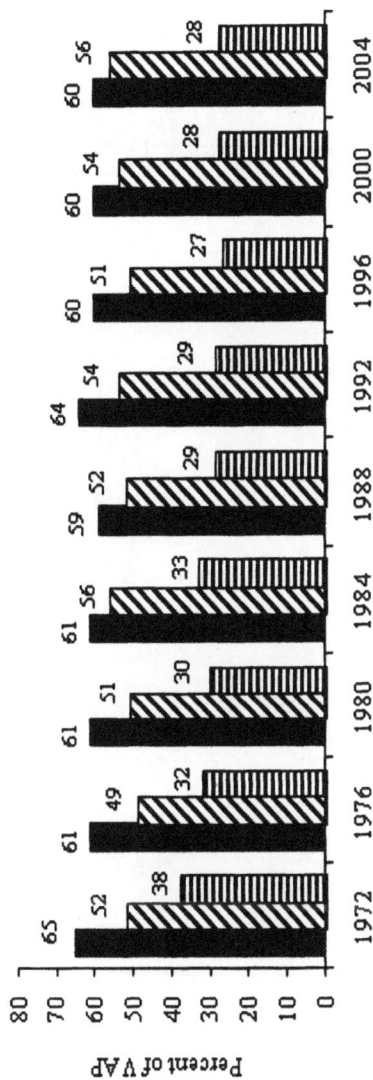

Source: Voting-Age Population (VAP), U.S. Bureau of the Census, Current Population Reports, 1992-2000, Hoadlette, 1992.

APPENDIX C

Latino Voter Turnout in Presidential Elections: 1972 to 2004

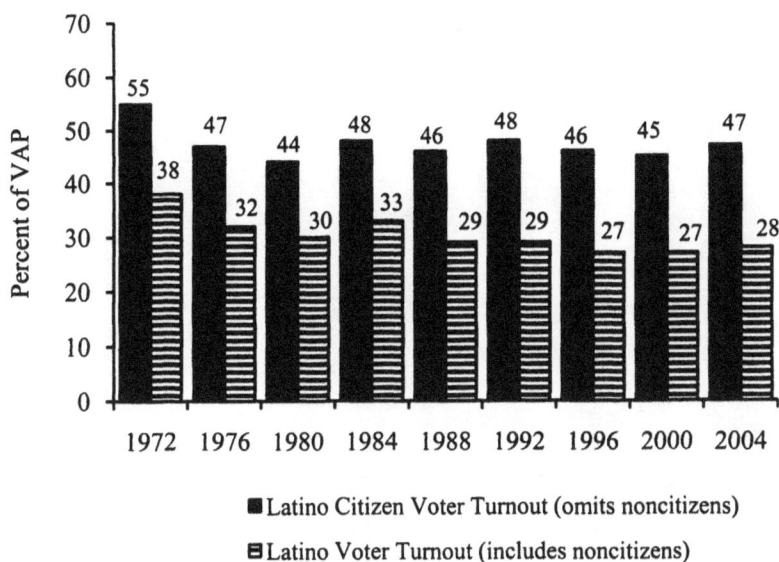

Source: Voting Age Population (VAP). Brischetto, 1992; and U.S. Bureau of the Census, Current Population Reports 1993, 1996, 1998, 2002, 2006. Latino citizen voter turnout numbers reported in Brischetto's paper were derived from the U.S. Census, Current Population Reports, Series P-90, *Voting and Registration in the November 1972-88 Election.*

APPENDIX D

State Estimates of Latino Registered Voters and Voter Turnout in the 2004 Presidential Election

State	Total VAP	Total CVAP	VAP	CVAP	Total Reg.	Reg.	Total Voted	Voted
NM	1,375	1,301	544	486	936	316	837	276
CA	26,085	20,693	8,127	4,433	14,193	2,455	12,807	2,081
TX	15,813	13,927	5,232	3,688	9,681	2,170	7,950	1,533
AZ	4,122	3,508	1,160	629	2,485	354	2,239	296
NV	1,699	1,477	301	151	965	83	871	72
FL	13,133	11,469	2,422	1,444	8,219	924	7,372	824
CO	3,398	3,109	574	361	2,307	204	2,097	165
NY	14,492	12,779	1,976	1,346	8,624	754	7,698	613
NJ	6,413	5,591	906	475	4,085	331	3,693	277
IL	9,303	8,640	1,031	608	6,437	343	5,672	294
US	215,694	197,005	27,129	16,088	142,070	9,308	125,736	7,587

*Numbers in thousands. VAP (Voting-Age Population); Pop. (Population); Reg. (Registration); Cit. (Citizen).   Percent of Latino Population—New Mexico, 44 percent, California and Texas, both with 36 percent, Arizona 29 percent, Nevada 24 percent, Florida and Colorado, both with 20 percent, New York and New Jersey, both with 16 percent and Illinois, 15 percent. Cit. (Citizen). Percent of Total Population data based on estimates of the Population of States by Race and

APPENDIX E Socioeconomic Characteristics of White, African American, Asian American, Native Americans, and Latino Populations				
Characteristics	Whites	Blacks	Asians	Latinos	Native Amer.
Population, 2006 (in thousands)					
U.S. Population	198.7	36.6	12.8	44.3	2.2
% of total	66.3	12.2	4.3	14.8	0.7%
Household Income Levels					
% of Incomes: $50,000 or less	40.5	58.8	35.3	57.6	------
% of Incomes: $50,000 to $99,999	34.2	28.2	32.1	30.1	------
% of Incomes: $100,000 or more	25.1	13.0	32.5	12.1	------
% living in poverty	8.2	24.3	10.3	20.6	27
Median household Income	$52,423	$31,969	$64,238	$37,781	33,762
Per Capita Income	$30,431	$17,902	$30,474	$15,421	--------
Education, 2003					
% Complete High School	89.4	80	87.6	57	AIA = 67 LOTA=73
% Receive B.A degree or more	30	17.3	49.8	11.4	AIA = 8.1 LOTA=13
Age, 2006					
% Under 18	23.8	29.6	22.8	33.7	29.3
% 18 to 64	62.7	62.0	68.2	60.8	62.8
% 65 and older	37.5	8.2	8.9	5.4	6.9
Median Age	39	31	35	27	AIA= 25 LOTA=30
Foreign-born, 2003					
% of population	3.9	7.4	67.8	40.2	1.5
% Naturalized Citizen	-----	4.5	34.4	11.2	-----
% Not a Citizen	-----	6.6	34.5	29.0	-----

Source: AIA= American Indian Areas, LOTA= Living outside Tribal Areas; The Native American population included Alaska Natives, U.S. Census 2004.

APPENDIX F
Latino Voters in the Presidential Elections: 1984 to 2004

Demographic Characteristics	Percent Reported Voting of VAP						
	1984	1988	1992	1996	2000	2004	AVG
Age							
18-24	18	16	16	16	15	20	17
25-44	28	24	24	20	23	23	24
45-64	43	34	37	36	38	39	38
65-74	47	50	42	49	51	47	48
Education							
9 years or less	21	16	14	15	14	12	15
High School	34	27	27	22	29	28	28
College: 4 + years	48	49	55	58	51	51	52
Family Income							
$9,999 or less	22	21	21	18	19	19	20
$10,000 to 14,999	25	20	15	17	20	15	19
$15,000 to 24,999	34	25	28	20	19	*	25
$35,000 to 49,999	48	50	48	35	32	*	43
$50,000 and over	56	64	55	52	47	48	54
Gender							
Female	33	30	31	29	30	31	31
Male	32	27	27	24	25	25	27

Source: U.S. Bureau of Census, 1993, 1989, 1993, 1998, 2002 and 2006.

APPENDIX G
Latino Voter Registration and Turnout in Arizona:
The 1992, 1996, 2000, and 2004 Presidential Elections

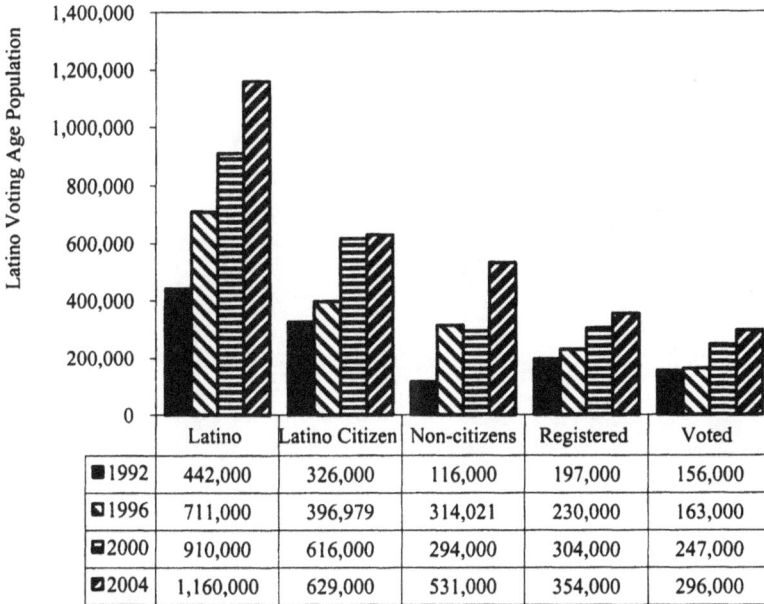

	Latino	Latino Citizen	Non-citizens	Registered	Voted
■1992	442,000	326,000	116,000	197,000	156,000
◨1996	711,000	396,979	314,021	230,000	163,000
▣2000	910,000	616,000	294,000	304,000	247,000
▨2004	1,160,000	629,000	531,000	354,000	296,000

	1992	1996	2000	2004
Arizona's VAP in thousands)	2,671	3,149	3,524	4,122
Percent of Latino VAP	17	23	26	28
Percent Registered of Citizen VAP	60	58	49	56
Percent Turnout of Citizen VAP	48	41	40	47
Percent Turnout of Latino Reg. Voters	79	71	81	84

Source: U.S. Bureau of the Census, "Voting and Registration in the
November 1992 Elections;" "Total--Voting-Age Population and Citizen
Voting-Age Population by Sex, for the United States and States: 2000."
"Reported Voting and Registration of the Total Voting-Age Population, by
Sex, Race and Hispanic Origin, for States: 2004;" and Voter Research
Institute, 1996. *Southwest Voter Research Notes.* Vol. X, No.1.

APPENDIX H

Method of Registration Among Arizona Residents, by Selected Characteristics

Method of Registration

Characteristics	County Clerk/ Election Office	Deputy Reg.	Mail-in Ballot	Voter Regs. Drive	Motor Vehicle Office	Other place/ way	DK	#	Total %
Race/Ethnicity									
White	19%	5%	12%	15%	18%	13%	17%	1,847	99%
Hispanic/Latino	21%	6%	13%	21%	8%	20%	10%	154	99%
Income									
Below $20,000	22%	6%	8%	16%	15%	18%	14%	352	99%
$22,000 And Over	19%	6%	13%	16%	18%	13%	15%	1170	100%
Education									
Non-High School Graduate	24%	6%	16%	14%	6%	13%	21%	126	100%
High School Grad.	21%	4%	11%	16%	16%	13%	19%	342	100%
College Graduate	20%	6%	12%	13%	19%	14%	17%	935	101%
Age									
18 to 29 Year Olds	16%	6%	8%	17%	18%	20%	15%	160	100%
30 Years and Older	23%	5%	9%	14%	15%	17%	18%	1124	101%
Party Identification									
Democrat	18%	6%	12%	19%	15%	14%	16%	684	100%
Republican	21%	6%	12%	14%	17%	13%	18%	976	101%
Independent	16%	4%	13%	16%	20%	14%	18%	385	101%

Characteristic	Strength Of Relationship	Chi Square	Significant
Race	Lambda = .600	.003	YES
Income	Gamma = .661	.049	YES
Education	Gamma = .694	.039	YES
Age	Gamma = .162	.322	NO
Political Party	Lambda = .448	.151	NO

Source: *The Arizona Poll*, February 1994, October 1994, February 1995, October 1996, February, 1997. Register/Registration (reg.); Don't Know (DK); Number (#); Percent (%).

BIBLIOGRAPHY

BOOKS

Abramson, Paul R., John H. Aldrich and David W. Rohde. 1994. *Change and Continuity in the 1992 Elections*. Washington, D.C.: CQ Press.

Alegre, Juan-Carlos, ed. 1992. *1991 National Roster of Hispanic Elected Officials*. Washington, D.C.: NALEO Educational Fund Inc.

Babbie, Earl. 1992. *The Practice of Social Research*. 6th ed. Belmont, CA: Wadsworth Publishing Co.

Barrera, Mario. 1979. *Race and Class in the Southwest*. Notre Dame: University of Notre Dame.

Bean, Frank, and M. Tienda. 1987. *The Hispanic Population of the United States*. New York: Russell Sage Foundation.

Berelson, Bernard R., Paul F. Lazarsfeld, and William N. McPhee. 1954. *Voting*. Illinois: The University of Chicago Press.

Berman, David R. 1992. *Reformers, Corporations, and the Electorate*. Colorado: University Press of Colorado.

Brischetto, Robert R. 1992. *Latino and the 1992 Presidential Election*. San Antonio, TX: Southwest Voter Research Institute Inc.

Burnham, Walter Dean. 1990. "The Turnout Problem." In *Classic Readings in American Politics*, edited by Pietro S. Nivola and David H. Rosenbloom. 2nd ed. New York: St. Martin's Press.

Campbell, Angus, Philip E. Converse, Warren E. Miller, and Donald E. Stokes. 1964. *The American Voter*, Michigan: University of Michigan Survey Research Center.

Conway, M. Margaret. 1991. *Political Participation in the Unites States*. Washington, D.C.: Congressional Quarterly Inc.

Davidson, Chandler. 1992. "The Voting Rights Act: A Brief History." In Bernard Gofman and Chandler Davidson, eds. *Controversies in Minority Voting*. Washington, D.C.: The Brookings Institution.

_____. 1989. *Minority Vote Dilution*. Washington, D.C.: Howard University Press.

De la Garza, Rodolfo O., Louis DeSipio, F. Chris Garica, John Garcia, and Angelo Falcon. 1992. *Latino Voices: Mexican, Puerto Rican, and Cuban Perspectives on American Politics*. Colorado: Westview Press.

Feagin, Joe R., and Clairece Booher Feagin. 1996. *Racial and Ethnic Relations*. New Jersey: Prentice Hall.

Gómez-Quiñones, Juan. 1994. *Roots of Chicano Politics, 1600–1940*. Albuquerque, N.M.: University of New Mexico Press.

_____. 1990. *Chicano Politics, Reality & Promise 1940–1990*. Albuquerque, N.M.: University of New Mexico Press.

Gonzalez, Juan. 2000. *Harvest of Empire: A History of Latinos in America*. New York: Penguin Books.

Greenberg, Edward S., and Benjamin I. Page. 1993. *The Struggle for Democracy*. New York: Harper Collins College Publishers.

Griswold Del Castillo, Richard. 1990. *The Treaty of Guadalupe Hidalgo: A Legacy of Conflict*. Oklahoma: University of Oklahoma Press.

Hellinger, Daniel, and Dennis R. Judd. 1994. *The Democratic Facade*. California: Wadsworth Publishing Company.

Hero, Rodney E. 1992. *Latinos and the U.S. Political System*. Philadelphia: Temple University Press.

Holder, Angela Roddey, and John Thomas Roddey Holder. 1987. *The Meaning of the Constitution*. New York: Barron's Educational Services, Inc.

Janda, Kenneth, Jeffery M. Berry, and Jerry Goldman. 2001. *The Challenge of Democracy*. 4th ed. New York: Houghton Mifflin Co.

Kanellos, Nicolás, ed. 1994. *The Hispanic-American Almanac* Vol. II. Detroit, MI.: Gale Research.

Phillips, Kevin P., and Paul H. Blackman. 1975. *Electoral Reform and Voter Participation*. Washington, D.C.: American Enterprise Institute for Public Policy Research.

Piven, Frances Fox, and Richard A. Cloward. 1988. *Why Americans Don't Vote*. New York: Pantheon Books.

Sabato, Larry J. 2001. *Overtime!* New York: Longman Pearson Education.

Sanchez, George I. 1967. *Forgotten People*. New Mexico: Calvin Horn Publisher Inc.

Samora, Julian, ed. 1966. *La Raza: Forgotten Americans*. Notre Dame: University of Notre Dame Press.

Spring, Joel. 2001. *Deculturalization and the Struggle for Equality*. New York: McGraw-Hill Inc.

Stanley, Harold W., and Richard G. Niemi. 2000. *Vital Statistics on American Politics 1999–2000*. Washington, D.C.: Congressional Quarterly.

Teixeira, Ruy. 1992. *The Disappearing American Voter*. Washington D.C.: Brookings Institution.

Valencia, Reynaldo A., Sonia R. Garcia, Henry Flores, and Jose Roberto Juarez Jr. 2004. *Mexican Americans and the Law*. Tucson, Arizona: The University of   Press.

Verba, Sidney and Norman H. Nie. 1972. *Participation in America: Political Democracy and Social Equality*. New York: Harper and Row Publishers.

Verba, Sidney, Kay Lehman Schlozman, and Henry E. Brady. 1995. *Voice and Equality Civic Voluntarism in American Politics*. Massachusetts: Harvard University Press.

Vigil, Maurilio E. 1987. *Hispanic in American Politics*. Maryland: University Press of America.

Walton, Hanes Jr., and Robert C. Smith. 2000. *American Politics and the African American Quest for Universal Freedom*. New York: Addison Wesley Longman Inc.

Welch, Susan, and John Comer. 1988. *Quantitative Methods for Public Administration*, 2nd ed. Pacific Grove, CA: Brooke/Cole Publishing Co.

Wolfinger, Raymond E., and Steven J. Rosenstone. 1980. *Who Votes?* New Haven: Yale University Press.

Yin, Robert K. 1994. *Case Study Research*. 2nd ed. Thousand Oaks, CA: Sage Publications Inc.

Government Documents

Arizona Secretary of State. 1991. "Research Figures for Motor Voter." Phoenix, Arizona.
_____. Task Force Meeting: National Voter Registration Act (NVRA). 20 October 1993. Phoenix, Arizona.
_____. *Task Force Meeting: Public Assistance Agency Group.* 17 November 1993. Phoenix, Arizona.
_____. *Task Force Meeting: National Voter Registration Act (NVRA).* 1 December 1993. Phoenix, Arizona.
_____. *Task Force Meeting: Summary of Subcommittees Reports.* 14 December 1993. Phoenix, Arizona.
_____. *Task Force Meeting: National Voter Registration Act Interim Committee.* 14 June 1994. Phoenix, Arizona.
_____. 1994. *Task Force Report: National Voter Registration Act of 1993.* Phoenix, Arizona.
_____. 1994. *Offer of Voter Registration.* Form NVRA-5. Phoenix, Arizona.
_____. 1995. *Reporting Requirements Under the NVRA.* Phoenix, Arizona.
_____. 1999. *NVRA Reporting Form 1998.* Phoenix, Arizona.
_____. 2001. *NVRA Reporting Form 2000.* Phoenix, Arizona.
Arizona. 1992. *Revised Statutes, Annotated.* St. Paul, Minn.: West Publishing Co.
_____. 1994. *Revised Statutes, Annotated.* St. Paul, Minn.: West Publishing Co.
Arizona. State Senate. Committee on Transportation. *S. B. 1295—Driver's License: Omnibus Revisions.* 18 February 1993. Phoenix, Arizona.
_____. State Senate. Committee on Transportation. *Fact Sheet: S. B. 1295—Driver's License: Omnibus Revisions.* 15 February 1993. Phoenix, Arizona.
Arizona Department of Economic Security. 1995. *State of Arizona: Population by Race/Sex Ethnicity: July 1, 1990, 1991, 1992.* Phoenix, AZ: Population Statistics Unit.
Arizona State Data Center. 1991. "Hispanic Origin and Race for Arizona Counties and Places." *1990 Census of Population and Housing* P.L. 94–171. Washington D.C.: U.S. Government Printing Office.
Commission on Civil Rights. 1988. *Barriers to Registration and Voting: An Agenda for Reform.* Washington, D.C.: Citizen's Commission on Civil Rights.
Council of State Governments. 1994. *The National Voter Registration Act of 1993 Manual.* KY: Lexington.
Crocker, Royce. 1994. *Voter Registration and Turnout: 1948–1992.* Washington, D.C.: Congressional Research Service, Library of Congress.
_____. 1994. *Voter Registration and Turnout For Each State: 1948–1992.* Washington, D.C.: Congressional Research Service, Library of Congress.
Federal Election Commission. 1994. *Implementing the National Voter Registration Act of 1993: Requirements, Issues, Approaches, and Examples.* Washington, D.C.: The National Clearinghouse on Election Administration.
Griffin, D. Rodman. 1992. "Hispanic Americans: Can They Find Economic Prosperity and Political Power?" *CQ Researcher* 2: 929–952.

The Hispanic Policy Development Project. 1984. *The Hispanic Almanac*. Washington, D.C.: The Hispanic Policy Development Project.

U.S. Bureau of the Census. 1972. Statistical Abstract of the United States: 1972 (89th edition). Washington, D.C.: U.S. Government Printing Office.

_____. 1976. Statistical Abstract of the United States (97th edition). Washington, D.C.: U.S. Government Printing Office.

_____. 1980. Statistical Abstract of the United States: 1980 (101st edition). Washington, D.C.: U.S. Government Printing Office.

_____. 1980. "The Hispanic Population in the United States: 1980." *Current Population Reports*. Washington, D.C.: U.S. Government Printing Office.

_____. 1984. "Special Studies: Voting and Registration Highlights from the Current Population Survey: 1964 to 1980." *Current Population Reports*, Series P-23, No.131. Washington, D.C.: U.S. Government Printing Office.

_____. 1984. Statistical Abstract of the United States: 1984 (104th edition). Washington, D.C.: U.S. Government Printing Office.

_____. 1987. Statistical Abstract of the United States: 1988 (108th edition). Washington, D.C.: U.S. Government Printing Office.

_____. 1991. "The Hispanic Population in the United States: March 1991." *Current Population Reports*, Series P-20, No. 455. Washington, D.C.: U.S. Government Printing Office.

_____. 1992. Statistical Abstract of the United States: 1992 (112th edition). Washington, D.C.: U.S. Government Printing Office.

_____. 1993. "Voting and Registration in the Election of November 1992." *Current Population Reports*, Series P20-466. Washington, D.C.: U.S. Government Printing Office.

_____. 1996. *Statistical Abstract of the United States: 1996*. U.S. Department of Commerce (116th edition). Washington, D.C.: U.S. Government Printing Office.

_____. 2001. Statistical Abstract of the United States: 2001 (121st Edition). Washington, D.C.: U.S. Government Printing Office.

_____. 2004. Statistical Abstract of the United States: 2004–2005 (124th Edition). Washington, D.C.: U.S. Government Printing Office.

_____. 2005. Statistical Abstract of the United States: 2006 (125th Edition). Washington, D.C.: U.S. Government Printing Office.

_____. 1998. "Voting and Registration in the Election of November 1996." *Current Population Reports*, Series P20-504. Washington, D.C.: U.S. Government Printing Office.

_____. 2001. "Counties Ranked by Numeric Population Change: 1990 to 2000." *U.S. Census Bureau, Census 2000 Redistricting Data* (P.L. 94-171). Washington, D.C.: U.S. Government Printing Office.

_____. 2001. "States Ranked by Percentage Population Change: 1990 to 2000." *U.S. Census Bureau* (PHC-T-2). Washington, D.C.: U.S. Government Printing Office.

_____. 2001. "The Hispanic Population in the United States." *Current Population Reports*, Series P20-535. Washington, D.C.: U.S. Government Printing Office.

_____. 2000. "Coming to America: A Profile of the Nation's Foreign Born." *U.S. Department of Commerce,* CENBR/00-2. Washington, D.C.: U.S. Government Printing Office.

_____. 2002. "Voting and Registration in the Election of November 2000." *Current Population Reports,* Series P20-542. Washington, D.C.: U.S. Government Printing Office.

_____. 2005. "Voting and Registration in the Election of November 2004." *Current Population Reports,* Series P20-556. Washington, D.C.: U.S. Government Printing Office.

_____. 2006. Table 1: Annual Estimates of the Population for the United States Regions, and States and for Puerto Rico: April 1, 2000 to July 1, 2006. Population Division, Washington D.C.: U.S. Government Printing Office.

_____. 2006. Nation's Population One-Third Minority. Population Division. Washington, D. C.: U.S. Government Printing Office.

_____. 2006. "Voting and Registration in the Election of November 2004." *Current Population Reports,* Series P20-556. Washington, D.C.: U.S. Government Printing Office.

U. S. Congress. House. *Voter Registration: Testimony from Helen I. Hudgens, Recorder, Coconino County, Arizona.* Subcommittee on Elections of the Committee on Hous Administration. 100th Congress, 2nd Session, 1989. Washington, D.C.: U.S. Government Printing Office.

_____. House. *Public Law 103-31.* 103d Congress, 1st Session, 1993. 107 Stat., Washington, D.C.: U.S. Government Printing Office.

_____. House. "The Impact of the National Voter Registration Act of 1993 on the Administration of Elections for Elected Office, 1993–1994." Federal Election Commission Report. July 1995.

"Voter Registration Reform: Pros & Cons." 1993. *Congressional Digest.* Washington, D.C: U.S. Government Printing Office.

"We the Americans...Hispanics." 1993. *U.S. Department of Commerce.* Washington, D.C.: U.S. Government Printing Office.

ON-LINE PUBLICATIONS

Ace Electoral Knowledge Network. "Comparing How Countries Run Elections." Retrived May 2007. http://aceproject.org/epic-en/vr.

"Arizona's English-only Law Ruled Unconstitutional." *CNN on the Web.* 29 April 1998. www.cnn.com.

Arizona Secretary of State. "2000 General Election Ballot Measures." *Arizona Secretary of State on the Web.* 3 August 2000. www.sosaz.com/election/ general/ 2000/ ballotmeasures.htm.

_____. "State of Arizona Official Canvass 2000 General Election: November 7, 2000." *Arizona Secretary of State on the Web.* 27 November 2000. www.sosaz.com/election//2000/General/Canvass2000GE.pdf.

Cano, Mistique. "Civil Rights Coalition Celebrates Renewal of Landmark Voting Rights Act." 27 July 2006. www.renewthevra.org.

"Census Figures Show Dramatic Growth in Asian, Hispanic Populations." *CNN on the Web.* 30 August 2000. www.cnn.com/2000/US/08/30/minority.population. html.

Collings Anthony. "Rejection seen for English-only Measure." *CNN on the Web.* 4 December 1996. http://coloquio.com/english/cnneng.html.

"Comprehensive VRA Timeline." *Voting Rights Act: Renew. Restore.* October, 2007. www.votingrights.org/timeline.

Federal Election Commission. *National Voter Turnout in Federal Elections: 1960–1996.* Retrieved March 9, 1997, from the Elections and Voting database, www.fec.gov/pages/htmlto5.htm.

_____. "The Impact of the National voter Registration Act of 1993 on the Administration of Federal Elections." June 1997. Retrieved July 27, 2000, from the Elections and Voting database, www.fec.gov/ votregis/ nvrasum.htm.

_____. "2000 Official Presidential General Election Results." *Federal Election Commission on the Web.* 20 June 2001. http://fecweb1.fec.gov/pubrec/ 2000presgeresults.htm.

_____. "2000 Presidential Electoral and Popular Vote." In *Federal Election 2000* on the Elections and Voting database, www.fec.gov/pubrec/fe2000/ elecpop.htm.

Garcia Olivia Reyes. "Latino Voter Turnout up 20 Percent." *The Bakersfield Californian on the Web.* 27 November 2000. www.bakersfield.com.

International Institute for Democracy and Electoral Assistance, "Voter Turnout Since 1945," retrieved May 2007, www.idea.int/publications/, p.84. www.idea.int /publications/vt/upload/VT_screenopt_2002.pdf

"Newly-Naturalized Latinos Inspired by Opportunity to Vote and are Ready to Participate." NALEO Educational Fund. 28 October 1996. www.naleo.org/ press/ surweb.html.

Pintor , Rafael López, Maria Gratschew, Jamal Adimi, Julie Ballington, Craig Brians, Sergei Lounev, Dieter Nohlen, Pippa Norris, Smita Notosusanto, Kate Sullivan, and Edmundo Urrutia. "Voter Turnout Since 1945: A Global Perspective." Report by the International Institute for Democracy and Electoral Assistance (International IDEA) 2002, Retrived May 2007. www.idea.int/publications/vt/ upload/VT_screenopt_ 2002.pdf.

Reese R. "Language Diversity and the Politics of the English Only Movement in the U.S." Paper presented at the 34th World Congress of the International Institute of Sociology, Tel. Aviv, Israel. 10 July 1999. www.csupomona.edu.

"Secretary of State Betsey Bayless Releases Statewide Voter Registration Figures for October 2001." Press release. 24 October 2001. www.sosaz.com/releases/ pressrelease85.htm.

"The Language Minority Provisions of the Voting Rights Act." *U.S. Department of Justice Civil Rights Division Voting Section on the WEB.* 11 February 2000. www.usdoj.gov/crt/voting/sec_203/activ_203.htm.

U.S. Bureau of the Census. 1973. "Voting and Registration in the Election of November 1972." Current Populations Report (P20-253). U.S. Bureau of the Census on the Web: www.census.gov/population/www/socdemo/voting/p20-253.html.

_____. 1978. "Voting and Registration in the Election of November 1976." Current Populations Report (P20-322). *U.S. Bureau of the Census on the Web.* www.census.gov/population/www/socdemo/voting/p20-322.html.

_____. 1982. "Voting and Registration in the Election of November 1980. Current Populations Report (P20-370). *U.S. Bureau of the Census on the Web.* www.census.gov/population/www/socdemo/voting/p20-370.html.

_____. 1986. "Voting and Registration in the Election of November 1984." Current Populations Report (P20-405). *U.S. Bureau of the Census on the Web.* www.census.gov/population/www/socdemo/voting/p20-405.html.

_____. 1989. "Voting and Registration in the Election of November 1988. Current Populations Report (P20-440). *U.S. Bureau of the Census on the Web.* http://www.census.gov/population/www/socdemo/voting/p20-440.html.

_____. 1997. *Money Income in the United States: 1997.* Retrieved July 12, 1999, from the Current Populations Report: Consumer Income P60-200, U.S. Census database, www.census.gov/ prod/3/98pubs/p60-200.pdf.

_____. 1997. *Poverty in the United States: 1997.* Retrieved July 12, 1999, from the Current Populations Report: Consumer Income P60-201, U.S. Census database, www.census.gov/ prod/ 3/98 pubs/p60-201.pdf.

_____. 1998. "Voting and Registration in the Election of November 1996. Current Populations Report (P20-504). *U.S. Bureau of the Census on the Web.* www.census.gov/population/www/socdemo/voting/p20-504.html.

_____. 1999. "Population Projections for States, by Age, Sex, Race and Hispanic Origin: 1995 to 2025." *U.S. Bureau of the Census on the Web.* www.census.gov.

_____. 1999. "States Ranked by Hispanic Population in 1998," *U.S. Census on the Web.* 15 September 1999. www.census.gov/population/estimates/ state /rank/ strnktb5.txt.

_____. 2001. "Profiles of General Demographic Characteristics 2000." *U.S. Census on the Web.* www.census.gov/prod/cen2000/index/html.

_____. 2001. "Profiles of General Demographic Characteristics: 2000 Census of Population and Housing, Arizona." *U.S. Census on the Web.* www.census.gov/prod/cen2000/dp1/2kh04.pdf.

_____. 2002. "Voting and Registration in the Election of November 2000 (P20-556)." U.S. Bureau of Census on the Web. http://www.census.gov/population/www/ socdemo/voting/p20-542.html.

_____. 2004. "Total--Voting-Age Population and Citizen Voting-Age Population by Sex, for the United States and States: 2000." *U.S. Census on the Web.* www.census.gov/population/ cen2000/ phc-t31/tab01-01.pdf.

_____. 2004. U.S. Interim Projections by Age, Sex, Race, and Hispanic Origin. *U.S. Census on the Web.* Retrieved June 2006. www.census.gov/ipc/www/usinterimproj/.

_____. 2005. "Reported Voting and Registration, by Race, Hispanic Origin, Sex, and Age, for the United States: November 2004." *U.S. Census on the Web.* www.census.gov/population/www/ socdemo/voting/cps2004.html

_____. 2007. "Annual Estimates of the Population by Sex, Race, and Hispanic or Latino Origin for the United States: April 1, 2000 to July 1, 2006." *U.S. Census on the Web.* http://www.census.gov/ipc/www/usinterimproj/.

_____. 2007. "Nativity: Middle Series, 1999 to 2100." *U.S. Bureau of Census on the Web.* www.census.gov/population/projections.

The Center for Voting and Democracy. "Presidential Election Voter Turnout: 1924 2000." *The Center for Voting and Democracy on the Web.* 22 October 2001. www.fairvote.org/turnout/preturn.htm.

The Political Reference Almanac. "Congressional Districts by State." *The Political Reference Almanac on the Web.* 2001. <www.polisci.com/legis/district/ AZ01.htm.

McDonlad, Michael. "2004 Voting-Age and Voting-Eligible Population Estimates and Voter Turnout." *U.S. Election Projection on the Web.* August, 2007. http://elections.gmu.edu/Voter_Turnout_2004.htm.

Yeager Holly. "Prop. 209 Proponent Takes His Campaign to the Nation." *Latino Link on the Web.* 3 August 1997. <www.latinolink.com/news.htm.

"2000 Election Ballot Measure Results." *Ballot Watch on the Web.* 10 November 2000. www.ballotwatch.org.

"2000 Official Presidential General Election Results." *Federal Election Commission on the Web.* 20 June 2001. http://fecweb1.fec.gov/pubrec/ 2000presgeresults.htm.

NEWSPAPERS

"Bilingual Foes Grid for Ballot." *The Daily Sentinel.* 10 September 2000.

"Bills, Bills, Bills." *The Phoenix Gazette.* 8 February 1989: A4.

Bingham, Maren. "Mahoney Eager to Start New Secretary of State Sees Many Changes." *The Phoenix Gazette.* 7 November 1990: A4.

Chichester, Martin S. "Easier to Vote." *The Phoenix Gazette.* 29 September 1988: A14.

"Constituent Communications Limit Advances in Election-Reform Fight." *Arizona Capitol Times.* 10 April 1991: Pg. 3–4.

"Disabled Urged to Register to Vote." *The Arizona Republic.* 2 September 1988: B8.

"Don't let These Bills Die." *The Phoenix Gazette.* 9 June 1990: A12.

"Drive Targets Disabled Voters." _The Arizona Republic._ 1 September 1988: B2.

"Ed Buck Seeks Open Primaries, Election-day Voter Registration." *The Arizona Republic.* 24 April, 1989: B1.

"Election 'Reform' Hot Topic; Registration Date Leads List." *Arizona Capitol Times.* 3 January 1990: section: front.

"Election-Reform Package Bogs Down in Senate." *Arizona Capital Times.* 11 April 1990: pg.1–2.

"Elections & Electors." *Arizona Capital Times.* 12 February 1990: pg.10–13.

Flannery, Pat. "Same-day Registration gets Shumway Support." *The Phoenix Gazette.* 7 April 1990: B1.

_____. "Election Reforms Bill Signed." *The Phoenix Gazette.* 2 July 1991: B1.

_____. "Panel to Propose Campaign Reforms Governor Might Make Own Suggestions." *The Phoenix Gazette.* 12 July 1991: B12.

"Good-Voting Habits Target of Program." *The Arizona Republic.* 25 March 1988: pg. 5–7.

Griffin, Sean. "Voter Sign-up Bill Gets Tentative OK Measure Relaxes Restrictions." *The Phoenix Gazette.* 5 April 1991: A6.

Harris, Don. "Shumway, Challenger Marked by Contrasts." *The Arizona Republic.* 27 August 1990, B1.

"House Approves Bill on Registering to Vote by Mail." The Arizona Republic 22 June 1991: A10.

Lavelle, Jack. "12-Year Limit For Lawmakers Sought." *The Phoenix Gazette.* 7 February 1990: A1.

_____. "Plan Would Ease Voter Registration." *The Phoenix Gazette.* 20 February 1990: B1.

"Legislature In Brief. *The Arizona Republic.* 16 March 1991: B2.

"Loud and Strong Recall Credited as County Voter List Swells." *The Phoenix Gazette.* 20 April 1988: A1.

"Maricopa County Recorder Hopefuls Vow to 'Clean Up' Voter Registration Rolls." *The Arizona Republic.* 6 November 1988: VG15.

McCloy, Mike. "Secretary of State Announces Bid For Election." *The Phoenix Gazette.* 3 January 1990: B1.

"Navajos Lack Voting Rights, U.S. Suit Says." *The Arizona Republic.* 9 December 1988, A1.

"Official Running for State Post that Mofford Gave Him in 1988." The Arizona Republic 4 January 1990: B3.

Padgett, Mike. "Mail-In Voter Registration Mulled Bill Would Ease Sign-Up, Save Money, Correct Inaccurate Rolls." *The Phoenix Gazette.* 8 June 1991: A8.

_____. "Invalid Voter Registrations Cost State." *The Phoenix Gazette.* 14 September 1990. A1.

_____. "Shumway Has No Time to Ease Into New Post Plans Several Changes in Elections Job." *The Phoenix Gazette.* 3 December 1990: B1.

"Party Activists, Former Officials to Study Problems in County Elections Operation." *The Phoenix Gazette.* 15 December 1988: B9.

"Planned Parenthood Registering Voters." *The Phoenix Gazette.* 4 July 1988: 2SB.

"Reform Urged to Rid Voter Roll Deadwood." *The Arizona Republic.* 18 September 1988: B1.

Sowers, Carol and Jim Walsh. "A Lesson in Getting Out Vote Minnesota Cuts Red Tape Election '90." *The Arizona Republic.* 17 July 1990: A1.

"Study: Arizona Tops U.S. in Registration Increase." *The Phoenix Gazette..* 7 November 1988. A1.

"State's Miles of Red Tape Driving License Applicant to Despair." *The Arizona Republic.* 24 February 1989: B1.

"Voters Numbers: Same Old Story." *Arizona Capital Times.* 15 April 1990: Pg. 3.

"Voter Purge Repealed with Republican (!) Help." *Arizona Capital Times.* 26 June 1991: Pg. 5–6.

"Voter Reforms." *Arizona Capitol Times.* 24 April 1991.

"Voter Registration Process can be Made Easier Yet." *The Arizona Republic.* 1 July 1990: C4.

"Voter Turnout Expected to Continue Low Trend." *The Arizona Republic.* 8 November 1988: A1.

"Wide-Open Voter Registration Pushed by Activist Coalition." *Arizona Capitol Times.* 21 February 1990: vol. 91, issue 5, pg. 1–2.

Yozwiak, Steve. "Two-Pronged Campaign is Launched to Allow Voter Registration." *The Arizona Republic.* 20 February 1990: CL10.

_____. "Measure to Ease Limits on Campaign Gift Gains." *The Arizona Republic.* 10 March 1990: B1.

_____. "Registering: Bump on Road to Polls 'Motor Voter' Helps Expand Rolls Election." *The Arizona Republic.* 16 July 1990: A1.

_____. "Mail-In Registration for Voters Is Backed." 16 May 1991: B13.

_____. "Reply to 'AzScam' Legislation OK'd Lobbyist Reins As Key Reform." The Arizona Republic. 10 November 1991: A1.

_____. "Governor Runoff Set For Feb. 26 U.S. Approval of Election Law is Expected," *The Arizona Republic.* 20 November 1990: A1.

ARTICLES, JOURNALS, SERIES PUBLICATIONS

Affigne, Tony. 2000. "Latino Politics in the United States: An Introduction." *Political Science & Politics* Vol. 33, no. 3 (September), pp. 523-527.

American Association of Motor Vehicle Administrators. "Administration, Terms, and Age Requirements for State Driver Licenses." January 1, 1996, pp. 1–2.

Calvo, Maria Antonia and Steven J. Rosenstone. 1989. *Hispanic Political Participation.* San Antonio, TX: Southwest Voter Research Institute.

Committee for the Study of the American Electorate. 1990. "Creating the Opportunity: Voting and the Crisis of Democracy." *Policy Studies Review* 9: 583–601.

Cotrell, Charles L. 1986. "Assessing the Effects of the U.S. Voting Rights Act." *Publius* 16, no. 4: 5–16.

Fenster, Mark J. 1994. "The Impact of Allowing Day of Registration Voting on Turnout in U.S. Elections From 1960 to 1992." *American Politics Quarterly* Vol.22, No.1 (January), pp. 74–87.

Franklin, Daniel P., and Eric E. Grier. 1997. "Effects of Motor Voter Legislation." *American Politics Quarterly* 25, no. 1:104–117.

Garcia, John A. 1986. "The Voting Rights Act and Hispanic Political Representation in the Southwest." *Publius* 16, no.4: 49–66.

Hero, Rodney E. 1993. "Questions and Approaches in Understanding Latino Politics: The Need for Clarification and Bridging." *National Political Science Review* 3: 153–157. Edited by Lucius J. Barker.

Jackman, Robert W. 1987. "Political Institutions and Voter Turnout in the Industrial Democracies." *American Political Science Review* 81, no. 2: 405–423.

Jackman, Robert W. and Ross A. Miller. 1995. "Voter Turnout in the Industrial Democracies During the 1980s." *Comparative Political Studies* 27, no. 4 (January): 467–492.

Knack, Stephen. 1995. "Does 'Motor Voter' Work? Evidence from State-Level Data." *The Journal of Politics* 57, no. 3: 796–811.

Mitchell, Glenn E. and Christopher Wlezien. 1995. "The Impact of Legal Constraints on Voter Registration, Turnout, and the Composition of the American Electorate." *Political Behavior* 17, no. 2: 179–202.

NALEO Education Fund. 1994. "An Overview of Hispanic Elected Officials in 1993." *The National Association of Latino Elected and Appointed Officials.* Washington, D.C.

_____. 2000. "Election 2000 Preview." Los Angeles, CA: NALEO.

Powell, G. Bingham, Jr. 1986. "American Voter Turnout in Comparative Perspectives." *American Political Science Review* 80, no. 1 (March): 17–43.

Rhine, Staci L. 1993. "Registration Reform and Its Relationship to Turnout in the American States." Ph.D. dissertation, Ohio State University.

_____. 1995. Registration reform and Turnout in the American States." *America Politics Quarterly* 23, no. 4 (October): 409: 426.

Sierra, Christine Marie, Teresa Carrillo, Louis DeSipio, and Michael Jones-Correa. 2000. "Latino Immigration and Citizenship." *Political Science & Politics* Vol. 33, no. 3 (September) pp. 535–540.

Solop, Fred and Susan Nicholls. 1986. *Motor Voter: Toward Universal Registration.* New York: Human SERVE.

Southwest Voter Research Institute. 1996. *Southwest Voter Research Notes.* Vol. X, No. 1. San Antonio, TX.

Verba, Sidney, Kay Lehman Schlozman, Henry Brady and Norman Nie. 1989. "A Study of the Voluntary Activity of the American Public in Politics, VoluntaryAssociations, Charities, and Religion." *The Citizen Participation Project.* National Science Foundation.

_____. 1993. "Race, Ethnicity and Political Resources: Participation in the United States." *British Journal of Politics* 23 (October): 453–497.

Wolfinger, Raymond E. and Jonathan Hoffman. 2001. 'Registering and Voting with Motor Voter." *Political Science & Politics* 32 (March): 85–92.

PERSONAL INTERVIEWS

Female. Election Director. Personal interview by Fred Solop. July 29, 1994.

Male. Election Director. Personal interview by Fred Solop. July 29, 1994.

Female. County Recorder. Personal interview by Elaine Rodriquez. June 17, 1996.

Male. Election Director. Personal interview by Elaine Rodriquez. June 17, 1996.

Female. Election Director. Personal interview by Elaine Rodriquez. June 18, 1996.

Male. Public Assistance Program Manager. Personal interview by Elaine Rodriquez. July 25, 1996.

Female. Public Assistance Program Supervisor. Personal interview by Elaine Rodriquez. July 25, 1996.

Male. Public Assistance Program Manager. Personal interview by Elaine Rodriquez. July 26, 1996.

Male. Public Assistance Program Regional Manager. Personal interview by Elaine Rodriquez. July 26, 1996.

Female. Executive Director for a National, Non-profit, Non-partisan Voter Registration Organization. Personal interview by Elaine Rodriquez. March 10, 1997.

PUBLIC HEARING

Public Hearing. "The National Voter Registration Act." Conducted by Margaret Steers, Donna Nolan, Jim Shumway, 13 December 1993. Central Library Auditorium, Phoenix, Arizona.

INDEX

Elaine Rodriquez, Ph.D., an Assistant Professor in the Department of Political Science and the Latino and Latin American Studies Program at Northeastern Illinois University (NEIU), 2003–2007; and a visiting Associate Professor at New Mexico Highlands University, 2007–2009. She is the co-creator of the Institute for Community Action Research (ICARE) in Chicago, a university/community partnership aimed at training Latino students on the mechanics of conducting research in their communities. Under I-CARE, she is the primary investigator on a project examining the civic and political levels of engagement of "soon-to-be" naturalized citizens. She has presented her research at various national conferences, including the American Political Science Association, Nuestra América in the United States, a U.S. Latino/a Studies Conference, and the Southwestern Political Science Association Conference. She is a coauthor of *The Status of Latinos in Chicago Public Schools: Dando un Paso, ¿Pa'Lante o Pa'Tras?,* a 2006 report.

www.ingramcontent.com/pod-product-compliance
Lightning Source LLC
Chambersburg PA
CBHW021820270326
41932CB00007B/275